Key issues in economics and business
The European Community

Key Issues in Economics and Business

Series editors: Alan Griffiths, Keith Pye and Stuart Wall

The European Community

Ian Barnes
with Jill Preston

Longman
London and New York

Longman Group UK Limited,
Longman House, Burnt Mill, Harlow,
Essex CM20 2JE, England
and Associated Companies throughout the world.

*Published in the United States of America
by Longman Inc., New York*

First published 1988
Second impression 1989

British Library Cataloguing in Publication Data
Barnes, Ian
   The European Community.– (Key issues
   in economics and business).
   1. European communities
   I. Title   II. Preston, Jill   III. Series
   337.1'42   HC241.2
   ISBN 0-582-29716-8

Library of Congress Cataloging in Publication Data
Barnes, Ian.
   The European Community/ Ian Barnes with Jill Preston.
      – (Key issues in economics and business)

   Bibliography: p.
   Includes index.
   ISBN 0-582-29716-8
   1. European Economic Community.   I. Preston, Jill   II. Title.
III. Series.
HC241.2.B293 1988
337.1=1 - dc19

Set in Linotron 202 10/11 pt Plantin
Produced by Longman Group (FE) Limited
Printed in Hong Kong

Contents

Part Two

Editors' preface

Each title in this series takes a particular area of economics or business studies and subjects it to rather more scrutiny than is possible in most introductory textbooks. Part one of each book concentrates on the key issues which present themselves for investigation or enquiry. It is hoped that a careful analysis of principle and data will save the reader considerable 'search time'. The issues selected will be those which are frequently the subject of examination questions at 'A' level, on professional courses and at the start of an undergraduate programme. Part two presents a range of examination questions to indicate the type of question the student is often expected to answer. The main objective will be to help students identify that part of their acquired knowledge which could be used in answering particular questions. A guide to sources of current information and data will help those who wish themselves to keep abreast of current developments or who intend to undertake essays/projects or dissertations in that particular area of economics or business.

Alan Griffiths
Keith Pye
Stuart Wall

Author's preface

Editor's preface

The European Community has been in existence for 30 years, in which time it has grown and developed into a major force in the world economy. At the same time the EC states have had an increasingly important voice in world affairs. Despite the fact that the United Kingdom has been a member of the Community since 1973, and nearly half of all trade is directed towards the EC, there is still a lack of understanding as how the EC works and its overall impact.

This book not only aims to improve the readers understanding of the Community, but it is also designed to assist those who wish to study the Community as part of formal study programmes. In order to directly assist in this process, a section containing sample questions is included.

I would like to thank all those who helped me with the preparation of the book, in particular my wife Pamela who did so much good work in checking the manuscript. A special thanks to the staff of the Commission Office and the European Parliament in London who provided so many useful documents. Also thanks to Michael Shackleton and Jimmy Young. Finally I would like to express my gratitude to Jill Preston who wrote chapter six on Regional Policy.

Ian Barnes
Humberside Business School

Acknowledgements

We are indebted to the following for permission to reproduce copyright material:

Agra Europe (London) Ltd. for table 9.3 from *Eurofish Report*, 27th January 1983; Paul Chapman Publishing Ltd. for table 10.2 (data) from *Southern Europe Transformed* by Allan Williams; The Economist Newspaper Ltd. for fig. 5.3 and table 9.2 from *The Economist* (12.4.86 & 28.8.76); Financial Times of London for table 8.1 from *Financial Times* (23.12.85); Gower Publishing Group for table 8.2 from p. 83 of *An Economic Analysis of Agriculture* (2nd Edition) by B. E. Hill and K. A. Ingersent; The Controller of Her Majesty's Stationery Office for tables 2.2 (*Future Financing of the Community*, 1984), 3.2 (*Overseas Trade Statistics*) and 3.3 (adapted from pp. 85–6 of *Developments in the European Community* July–December, 1986); International Council for the Exploration of the Sea for table 9.1 from *Cooperative Research Report* No. 37; Methuen & Co. for fig. 8.5 from fig. 4.1, p. 83 of *The Common Agricultural Policy: Past, Present and Future* by Brian E. Hill; Organisation for Economic Co-operation and Development, Paris for tables 1.1 (OECD *Economic Survey* 1986–87) & 10.5 (OECD *Report on Portugal* 1984); Oxford University Press for fig. 3.2 from p. 18 of *Economies of Scale, Competitiveness and Trade Patterns Within the European Community* by N. Owen; Erich Schmidt Verlag and Friedrich Reinecke Verlag for a map & table from 'The Community of Twelve 1986' from p. 3 of *The German Tribune* (1.2.87).

List of abbreviations

ACP	African, Caribbean and Pacific States
Benelux	The customs union that existed between Belgium, Luxembourg and the Netherlands
BRITE	Basic Research in Industrial Technology for Europe
CAP	Common Agricultural Policy
CCP	Common Commercial Policy
CCT	Common Customs Tariff
CET	Common External Tariff
CFP	Common Fisheries Policy
CMEA or Comecon	Council for Mutual Economic Assistance
COMET	Community Programme in Education and Training for Technology
COREPER	Committee of Permanent Representatives
DG	Directorate-General of the EC
EAGGF	European Agricultural Guidance and Guarantee Fund
EC	European Community
ECJ	European Court of Justice
ECSC	European Coal and Steel Community
ECU	European Currency Unit

EDC	European Defence Community
EDF	European Development Fund
EEC	European Economic Community
EEZ	Exclusive Economic Zone
EFTA	European Free Trade Area
EIB	European Investment Bank
EMCF	European Monetary Cooperation Fund
EMF	European Monetary Fund
EMS	European Monetary System
EMU	European Monetary Union
EPC	European Political Cooperation
ERDF	European Regional Development Fund
ERM	Exchange Rate Mechanism
ESC	Economic and Social Committee
ESF	European Social Fund
ESPRIT	European Research and Development in Information Technology
EUA	European Unit of Account
Euratom	European Atomic Energy Authority
FEOGA	European Agricultural Guidance and Guidance Fund
FTA	Free Trade Areas
GATT	General Agreement on Tariffs and Trade
GDP	gross domestic product
GNP	gross national product
GSP	Generalized System of Preferences
IATA	International Air Transport Association
ICES	International Council for the Exploration of the Seas

IMF	International Monetary Fund
INI	Institutor Nacional de Industria
MCA	Monetary Compensatory Amount
MEP	Member of the European Parliament
MFA	Multi-Fibre Arrangement
MSY	maximum sustainable yield
NATO	North Atlantic Treaty Organisation
NEAFC	North East Atlantic Fisheries Commission
NFU	National Farmers' Union
NIC	newly industrialised country
OECD	Organisation for Economic Cooperation and Development
OEEC	Organisation for European Economic Cooperation
OPEC	Organisation of Petroleum Exporting Countries
OSY	optimum sustainable yield
PO	producer organisations
RACE	Research and Development in Advanced Communication Technology for Europe
R&D	Research and Development
SAD	Single Administrative Document
SAP	Social Action Programme
STABEX	system for stabilising export earnings
TAC	total allowable catch
The Nine	Members of the EC after the first enlargement (the Six plus Denmark, Ireland and the United Kingdom)
The Six	The original members of the EC (Belgium, France, West Germany, Italy, Luxembourg, Netherlands)
The Ten	Members of the EC after the second enlargement (the Nine plus Greece)

The Twelve	The current membership of the EC (the Ten plus Spain and Portugal)
UA	unit of account
UK	United Kingdom
UN	United Nations
UNCLOS	United Nations Conference on the Law of the Sea
USA	United States of America
USSR	Union of Soviet Socialist Republics
VAT	value added tax
VER	Voluntary Export Restraint

Map of the Community of Twelve

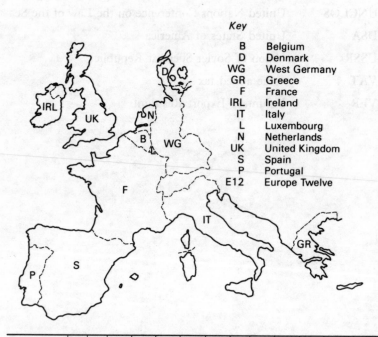

Key

B	Belgium
D	Denmark
WG	West Germany
GR	Greece
F	France
IRL	Ireland
IT	Italy
L	Luxembourg
N	Netherlands
UK	United Kingdom
S	Spain
P	Portugal
E12	Europe Twelve

	B	D	G	GR	F	IRL	IT	L	N	UK	S	P	E12
Population (million)	9.9	5.1	60.9	10.0	55.4	3.6	57.1	0.4	14.6	56.6	38.8	10.3	322.6
Area (thousand sq km)	31	43	249	132	544	70	301	3	41	244	505	92	2255
MEPs	24	16	81	24	81	15	81	6	25	81	60	24	518
Commission members	1	1	2	1	2	1	2	1	1	2	2	1	17
Votes in Council of Ministers	5	3	10	5	10	3	10	2	5	10	8	5	76

Source: The German Tribune, 1 February 1987, p 3

Part one

Chapter one
Introduction

Europe in the 1980s is a very different place to that which lay in ruins after the Second World War. Politically and economically it is now firmly divided into two camps. In the east, there are those countries which are members of the Council for Mutual Economic Assistance, usually known as Comecon. In the west, the European Community (EC) is predominant, with its membership of 12 countries and 320 million citizens. Although the members of the EC still retain their national independence, and are free to depart from the Community, the importance of the organisation has grown to such an extent that, for most, leaving is not now a serious item on the political agenda. Increasingly through trade, and because the EC is perceived to have a political purpose, member states are finding themselves drawn into an ever more intense relationship.

1.1   The search for a united Europe

The increasing degree of political and economic integration has come about as a result of an increased pace of industrialisation and trade. Technology transfers between economies has become essential, and there has developed a high degree of interdependence in terms of the supply of industrial products. Not only is autarky no longer a sustainable economic strategy, but there is an acceptance of the need to have highly developed political links. The failure to find satisfactory methods of resolving political disputes between nation states, caused two major European conflicts in the space of 30 years.

The destruction and waste of the two world wars led a number of people to believe that there must be a better way to organise European affairs. It was clear to them that the nation state as an organisation had failed to provide the peace and prosperity that was demanded of it, and so it should be replaced by a new structure, perhaps by a federal Europe. Federalism is an attempt to create a political union among separate states by dividing powers between a central authority and the member countries. In its most advanced form it would create a united states of Europe. Its major advantage is that there is the potential to develop a more efficient central authority, which would reduce conflict between its members because of its ability to promote shared interests. The former nation states would of course still retain certain powers, and still retain their cultural and social identities. Decision making should not be so centralised that the needs of particular regions would be ignored.

In 1947, Luxembourg, Belgium and the Netherlands agreed to the formation of the Benelux customs union which came into operation in 1948. Also in 1948, the Organisation for European Economic Cooperation (OEEC) was established, to help with the coordination of post-war American aid to Europe. In 1961, this intergovernmental organisation was reformed with a more world-wide membership, under a new title of the Organisation for Economic Cooperation and Development (OECD). This body still exists today, providing useful independent economic advice. The pressure to create a European assembly to promote both political and economic cooperation, led to the setting up of the Council of Europe in 1949. As an organisation for promoting federalism, it proved to be a disappointment, because it had no real power to do anything more than discuss issues. Today the Council of Europe still exists, sharing its accommodation in Strasbourg with the European Parliament

1.2 The formation of the European Community

The problem with grand strategies is that they tend to evaporate when faced with reality. Inevitably, the enthusiasm for a federal Europe declined as memories of the Second World War became less immediate, and more limited strategies became appropriate. In 1950, the French Foreign Minister, Robert Schuman, proposed the setting up of the European Coal and Steel Community (ECSC). This involved the placing of coal and steel production under a common High Authority. The importance of these materials in a strategic sense is easy to appreciate. The aim was to achieve rational production of these commodities in order to benefit all members. Six countries eventually signed the Treaty of Paris in 1951 to become members; they were; France, Germany, Italy,

Belgium, Luxembourg and the Netherlands. The UK declined membership partly on the basis that the Labour Government had only just nationalised this sector of the economy. Also, there was no great enthusiasm about participation in European integration among the British. The UK saw the Empire, and the special relationship it thought it had with the USA as a more important priority.

The ECSC was an attempt at economic integration within a limited geographic area, involving only a relatively small, but vital, area of the national economies of its members. It was of course hoped that it would lead to greater things. Attempts were made to launch a European Defence Community, and a European Political Community in the early 1950s, but these failed as the crisis of the Korean War passed. In order to pick up the pace of things, the foreign ministers of the Six met in Messina in 1955. They set up an intergovernmental committee to examine and propose further strategies for greater integration. What emerged from the process was a proposal to form a European Economic Community (EEC), and a European Atomic Energy Community (Euratom), both of which came into existence in 1958.

1.3   The UK and Europe

It soon became clear that the UK's decision to remain outside the Community was a mistake. The establishment of the European Free Trade Area (EFTA) as a rival organisation was only a limited success, as its members were largely on the periphery of Europe. The British were slow to see that there was little to be gained from sticking with many of their traditional markets and international loyalties. They saw EFTA as a way of minimising their commitment to Europe in that it was never envisaged as anything more than a convenient device to promote trading interests. The UK belatedly attempted to join the EC in 1961, and again in 1967 without success. Membership was not achieved until 1973, by which time, the UK was not able to hitch on to the dynamic growing economies of the EC, as the world economy had moved into a phase of slow growth. The terms of membership which the UK accepted were not favourable, and this was to cause many years of dispute. Unlike Ireland and Denmark, who gained substantially from the Common Agricultural Policy (CAP), the UK became a net contributor to the EC budget. Between 1 January 1973 and 31 December 1986, the UK's net contribution to the EC was £7,772 million, which represented a net payment of £1.52 million per day of membership. The body of law and practice (the so-called *aquis communautaire*) was disadvantageous to the UK. Much of the reason for this was that decisions had been made with the original Six in mind. This was to cause a state of friction between the EC and the UK, which became a permanent feature of decision making.

1.4   The Community in the 1980s

The 1980s saw an era of expansion of the Community, with the movement to the south. Greece became a member of the EC in 1981, followed by Spain and Portugal in 1986. This continued expansion reflects on the vitality of the Community, and demonstrates how dominant it has become in European affairs. The EFTA countries are now clients of the EC in economic affairs, and the Twelve are a trading entity which matches Japan and the

Table 1.1   Main economic indicators for the Community

	GDP per capita (US$) 1986		Average annual economic growth[1] 1981–85	Inflation %[2] 1986	Unemployment %[2] 1986
	Real*	Nominal†			
Belgium	11,300	11,300	0.6	4.6	12.9
Denmark	13,000	15,800	2.3	4.8	7.5
France	11,800	12,800	1.1	4.6	10.5
West Germany	12,900	14,700	1.3	3.9	8.1
Greece	6,100	3,900	1.0	22.6	7.6
Ireland	7,300	7,000	1.8	5.6	18.4
Italy	9,900	8,800	0.9	9.7	13.4
Luxembourg	14,300	13,900	2.4	5.4	1.3
Netherlands	11,800	11,900	0.7	0.4	12.0
Portugal	5,500	2,800	1.0	19.2	8.6
Spain	8,000	5,900	1.4	11.8	21.7
UK	11,400	9,600	1.9	3.9	12.0

Source: OECD and Eurostat GDP figures. Quoted by the *Financial Times*, 10 February 1987:

1. OECD Report Switzerland 1986/1987
2. Commission estimates published in *Annual Economic Report 1986–1987*.
* Converted at purchasing power parities.
† Converted at exchange rates.

United States in importance. The growth in its influence in trade and economic affairs, has not increased political integration to the extent that many hoped for at the start of the process. There was a hope that as tasks were transferred from the nation state to the Community, so citizens' loyalty would move towards the centre with its institutions such as the European Parliament and the Commission. This transition has not taken place, however, and little interest is shown by most citizens in EC affairs. Community decisions are still a reflection of the strength of national interests, and little thought is given to promoting a broader European interest.

Despite the continued pursuit of national self-interest by members, their ability to act independently of others has diminished. This interdependence is not restricted to economic affairs, it also applies to the physical environment. Even in political matters, states now feel it is important to take account of the views of Community partners over such issues as South Africa. Although European political cooperation is in its early stages, this diplomatic cooperation seems destined to develop as a joint European response is expected on international issues. This does not mean that a Community response will lead to joint action, for as in other areas of decision making the Community must move at the pace of the slowest and least committed.

The areas of economics and politics which the EC now influences is enormous, and it is impossible to cover them all within the scope of a limited text. What the text attempts to do is to select issues which are important in terms of the Community's current development. Some of these have been of concern for some time, for example the slowness of the decision-making process. The inability of the Community to resolve many of the pressing issues for reform in areas like the internal market will continue to be a source of concern, unless the Single European Act (see Appendix one) proves to be effective. Despite its decline in importance relative to the national income of the Twelve, agriculture is still the issue which dominates the agenda of the Community. Europe, after the Second World War, was a place where food was in short supply, now it is a surplus producer. The cost of supporting the industry drains the Community's finances to such an extent that much more useful projects are ignored or left underfunded. It also leads to accusations that the EC is disrupting world markets.

Among the new problems that the Community has had to face is how to cope with the recession and mass unemployment. This has caused a number of problems for the regional and industrial policies of the EC. Existing policies have had to be revised, and new strategies have had to be developed. To the fore in this area, are the initiatives to promote new technology, which attempt to act as a catalyst in promoting cooperation between European firms. Although it is too early to say if these schemes will work, there are areas where it is reasonable to claim some success, for example in the case of the European Monetary System (EMS) and, after many years of searching, the Common Fisheries Policy (CFP).

It is difficult to predict which areas will be of greatest concern in the future, but it is clear that a great deal of the Community's energy will be devoted to coping with the changes brought about by the most recent expansion to the south. Although the text considers this as a separate issue, it has implications for all areas of policy.

Chapter two
The tribulations of making up twelve minds

The EC is unusual in that, unlike other international organisations
to which nation states belong, it does not need to rely on moral
pressure to achieve its aims. It has a legislative process, and can
pass laws which apply directly in member countries. Not only does
the EC have a significant impact upon the operation of markets,
it can sometimes allocate money to achieve its policy aims. Also,
it has a judicial system which helps to ensure that its decisions are
carried out. The body of law and policy which has been developed
(*acquis communautaire*) is now considerable, and in a number of
areas the EC has developed a dynamic of its own.

Members of the EC are tied together in an unusually intense
relationship which some hope will eventually lead to a high degree
of political unity. Despite these long-term aspirations, the EC's
decision making is still firmly within the control of the nation states
which make up its membership. Each state pursues national objectives, and still regards success in terms of domestic electorates, who
are less easy to please in an era of slow growth. The strength of
national interest, the complexity of many of the issues and the
nature of the institutions makes for a decision-making process
which is facing continuing criticism on a whole variety of grounds.
Four particular criticisms are as follows:

1. The process is highly inefficient. There are over 400
   Commission proposals awaiting the decision of the Council of
   Ministers at any one time. Decision making is not only slow,
   very often no decision is reached at all.
2. Only minimal change is achieved because proposals get
   watered down, or involvement is limited, as in the case of the
   UK's only partial involvement in the EMS.
3. Many of the issues it spends a great deal of time on appear
   irrelevant or trivial, for example the harmonisation of lawn-
   mower emissions.

4. There is a lack of popular involvement in the process, and despite the existence of the European Parliament, there is no real democratic control.

To explain decision making in the EC and to understand how some of these criticisms have arisen, this chapter will examine first of all the role of institutions, then the policy formulation process and possible reforms to it. Finally, in order to illustrate the contentious nature of the process, a case study of reform of the EC's budget will be considered.

2.1 The institutions

The major institutions responsible for running the EC still have largely the same structure as when the Community was set up in 1958. They have of course had to adapt to the increased membership of the Community and naturally relationships have developed over time.

The Commission

The Commission is a hybrid organisation, in that it has a mixture of political and administrative tasks. Its main functions are upholding the European ideal, proposing new policy initiatives and ensuring that existing policies are implemented. Although the Commission employs around 15,000 people, in a narrow sense it is taken to be the 17 Commissioners who are directly nominated by the 12 member states. The United Kingdom, France, Germany, Italy and Spain, each nominate two members while the rest appoint only one each. Commissioners serve a four-year term. They are collectively responsible to the European Parliament, and can only be removed during their term of office by a censure motion carried by a two-thirds majority. There is no procedure to remove individual Commissioners. Each Commissioner is responsible for specific areas of work, for example, agriculture, social policy and so on. The Commission takes decisions by majority vote, and all are expected to support the decision.

The Council of Ministers

The Council is the expression of national interest in the EC and is its principal decision-making institution. Each country sends one ministerial delegate to its meetings. The minister involved depends on the subject under discussion; in 1984 there were 20 different types of Council ranging from agriculture to cultural affairs. Of the 80 Council meetings held in that year, 17 involved the foreign ministers (the most senior of Councils) and 14 concerned agricultural ministers, reflecting agriculture's importance to the Community. The Presidency of the Council is held for six months by each state in rotation.

Committee of Permanent Representatives

Often known as COREPER (the abbreviation of its French title) this is a body of national officials of ambassadorial rank, who have the task of discussing all proposals from the Commission and identifying areas of agreement and conflict. The Council of Ministers are unable to discuss the large number of proposals they receive in detail, so the Committee acts as a filter. To carry out the more detailed work, a number of permanent and *ad hoc* working parties also exist, for example, a committee on the budget. Although it has been in existence since 1958, the Committee was not formally institutionalised until the Merger Treaty of 1967. (This was the treaty which formally brought together the executives of the EEC, ECSC and Euratom.)

Decision making has normally to be by unanimous vote on all major issues, although there is a procedure for voting by weighted majority. Under this system, the UK, France, Germany and Italy have 10 votes each; Spain has 8 votes; Belgium, Greece, the Netherlands and Portugal have 5 votes each; Denmark and Ireland have 3 votes each; and Luxembourg 2. A proposal must obtain 54 votes out of the 76 to achieve a majority. This weighted majority system may become much more important in the enlarged Community, as Spain and Portugal may join with the other southern states and be able to act as a blocking minority, for example, when it comes to preventing the rejection of the European Parliament's amendments to the budget.

As a result of the Single European Act, there will be greater use of majority voting in the areas of the internal market, social policy, research and technological development, the environment and economic and social cohesion.

European Council

This is not an institution recognised by the treaties, but has developed since 1974 as the place where the big issues of principle in the EC are discussed. It is composed of the heads of state and government along with their foreign ministers. They meet three times per year – once in each of the countries holding the Presidency of the Council, and on a third occasion in Brussels.

European Parliament

Despite its name, the European Parliament is not a Parliament in the normal Western European sense in that it cannot initiate legislation, and it does not have the final say in passing laws. The Parliament does have the right to be consulted, and if the Council of Ministers fails to do so, legislation may be struck down. Parliament can question the Commission and can dismiss it as a body by a two-thirds majority. The power to dismiss the Commission is, however, so drastic that it is unlikely ever to be used and in any case it would have no say in the replacements; indeed they could be the same people.

The Parliament has significant powers in the area of the budget. In 1979 it first rejected the budget, and in 1984, 1985 and 1986 the budget was held up because of the activities of the Parliament. This militancy has resulted in the Parliament being able to influence significantly the levels of expenditure on the Social Fund and Regional Development Fund. As a result of the Single European Act, Parliament has the right to reject or amend legislation from the Council in cases where majority voting is involved. The Council then has to reconsider its position, but can only pass legislation unanimously if it wishes to ignore the Parliament. The practical implication of this change is unclear, but it does increase the voice of the Parliament, but at the expense of the speed of decision making.

It has 518 members who since 1979 have been directly elected. The United Kingdom, France, Germany and Italy have 81 members each, Spain 60, the Netherlands 25, Belgium, Greece and Portugal 24 each, Denmark 16, Ireland 15 and Luxembourg 6. Members are formed into political groups on a European-wide basis. The administration of the Parliament lies in Luxembourg, but plenary sessions are normally held in Strasbourg and committees meet in Brussels.

Economic and Social Committee

This is a consultative body made up of three groups; employers, trade unions and 'special interests' such as consumer organisations, progressions and so on. Although it must be consulted over certain issues, it is of only minor significance.

European Court of Justice

This body's function is to settle legal disputes involving Community law. There are 13 judges, including one from each country. Judges serve six-year terms. The Court's decisions apply directly in the member countries. For some the Court is the most important EC body because of its role in building up a web of legal judgments binding on countries and companies in the EC. It is very rare indeed to see its judgments directly defied.

2.2 The policy-making process

Almost every proposed item of legislation within the EC is graced with the title of policy. It is, however, difficult to identify what could easily be described as an identifiable strategy in many areas. What tends to emerge from the process is a series of initiatives which affect the member states in a number of different ways. Firstly, there are those which regulate the common market and, therefore, affect trading relations between members. Secondly, there are policies like agriculture and fisheries, where national policies have been substantially replaced by the EC. Thirdly, there are the cases where national policy is being supplemented by EC policy as in the case of regional and industrial policy. Fourthly, in areas like the EMS, the degree of participation depends on the member state. Finally, there are those areas which emerge as a cause of common concern.

Unlike most other international organisations, EC decisions directly affect domestic business, and policies tend to concern issues which have arisen in the past at a national level. National interest groups often have a clear opinion on issues as a consquence of this. Interest groups do operate at the Community level, and the Commission consults with many hundreds of them in the course of a year. In most cases, however, groups see national governments as champions of their various causes, relying very heavily on contact with specific ministries. Only in a few cases, like agriculture, could it be said that there were European-wide groups who speak with one voice.

National policy formation on EC issues tends to vary according to the country concerned. In the UK it is highly coordinated by the European Secretariat of the Cabinet Office. Negotiating stances tend to be worked out in advance, controlling the level of expenditure being regarded as a priority. By contrast, West Germany tends to be less coordinated, with ministries adopting separate positions. What seems to be common to most countries, with the exception of Denmark, is that national parliaments have far less control over their governments' conduct of EC affairs than is the case in almost any sphere of public policy. Where cash, or some important issue of commercial policy is at stake, governments have to appear to deliver. Especially in the UK, being too soft on the EC can be regarded as a major political weakness. This in turn means that reactions are anticipated at the Community level, so that policies are proposed which offer something for all.

In simple terms, decision making within the Community's institutions amounts to the Commission proposing, the European Parliament being consulted, and the final decision being taken by the Council of Ministers. When the process is completed, what emerges is one of the following:

1. *Regulations* – these are binding, and have direct effect in member states.
2. *Directives* – these are also binding, but the method of achieving the end result is up to the individual states, for example, levels of exhaust emission.
3. *Decisions* – these are obligatory on the government, enterprise or individual concerned.
4. *Recommendations and opinions* – these have no binding force.

Fig. 2.1 gives the relationship between the Community's institutions.

The enthusiasm with which the Commission has proposed bold new initiatives has waned over the years. This is partly because of repeated failures in the past, an increasing burden of administration and the growing power of the Council of Ministers. The real power lies firmly within the nationally based organisations. Member states can simply apply a veto where they feel that their essential national interests are threatened. This is the so-called 'Luxembourg Compromise', designed in 1966 to meet French objections to the erosion of national sovereignty. It means members agree to disagree over a particular proposal, and it simply remains on the table in a kind of legislative limbo. It is invoked not only by the Council of Ministers but in a *de facto* sense by the Permanent Representatives indicating that the veto will be applied at a later date. In order to overcome this veto, attempts are often made to package

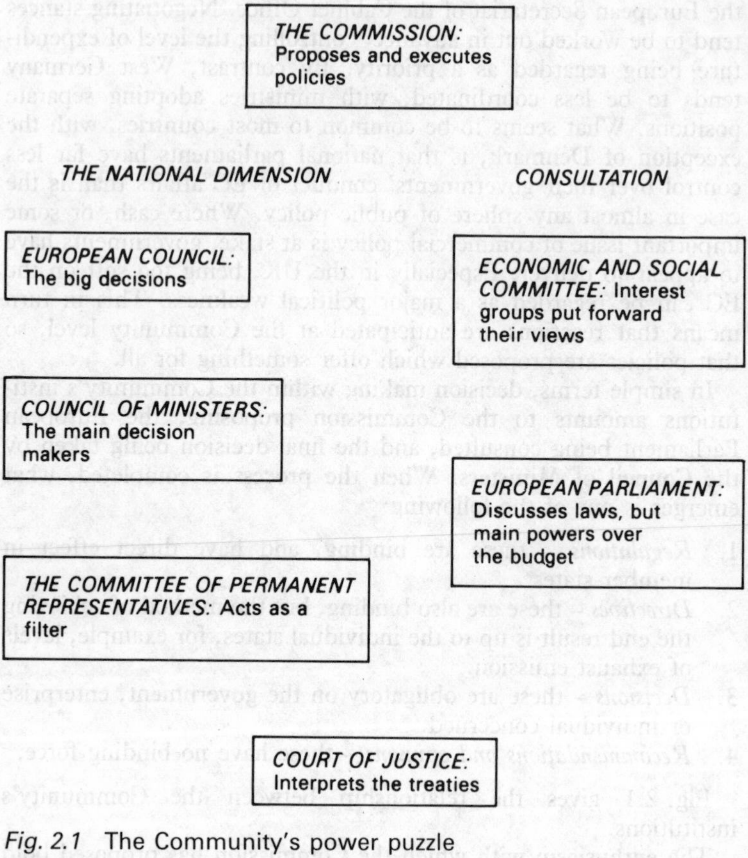

THE COMMISSION:
Proposes and executes policies

THE NATIONAL DIMENSION

CONSULTATION

EUROPEAN COUNCIL:
The big decisions

ECONOMIC AND SOCIAL COMMITTEE: Interest groups put forward their views

COUNCIL OF MINISTERS:
The main decision makers

EUROPEAN PARLIAMENT:
Discusses laws, but main powers over the budget

THE COMMITTEE OF PERMANENT REPRESENTATIVES: Acts as a filter

COURT OF JUSTICE:
Interprets the treaties

Fig. 2.1 The Community's power puzzle

proposals so that all member states can appear to have gained something from a set of proposals. It remains to be seen whether the use of majority voting will increase with the introduction of the Single European Act.

The place of the European Parliament in the process has in the past been marginal, although it is clearly starting to assert itself. It is still the case, however, that little tends to be heard about its deliberations, partly because they are not of sufficient importance, but also because being based in Strasbourg means that it is geographically remote from the centre stage of the Community's politics.

2.3 Reforms of the decision-making machinery

The Luxembourg Council of December 1985 agreed on limited reforms in the decision-making process, which resulted in the Single European Act. The powers of the European Parliament were increased, and the Council of Ministers is to increase the use of voting using the weighted majority system. These modest reforms may buy time for those who oppose any real erosion of national sovereignty. It seems unlikely that the demands for more fundamental reform will go away.

In particular, it has been suggested that there should be:

1. A more streamlined Commission – perhaps with only 12 or even 9 members.
2. An abandoning of the veto in all circumstances.
3. A European Parliament with the power to initiate legislation.
4. A bringing together of all institutions in one locality, preferably Brussels.

Few institutional changes are going to mean much, however, if nation states still insist in pursuing their national self-interest to the exclusion of a worthwhile Community position.

2.4 Policy implementation

Policy implementation is important, firstly because of the volume of policy which is now in existence. The Commission with its task of ensuring implementation has found this to be a source of increased power, although this is often ignored by commentators because the set-piece political conflicts are over. Most policy is actually administered by the member states with the Commission supervising its conduct. Non-compliance can be dealt with by final resort to the European Court of Justice (ECJ). However, inadequate supervision, insubstantial funds or a lack of national enthusiasm can just as easily frustrate policy intentions.

The second reason why implementation is important is because of the slowness of the policy process itself. Once a policy is in place, some member countries are reluctant to accept change because of the balance of advantage built up over a period of time. If the policy is particularly disadvantageous to others, or to the Community as a whole, it is difficult to reverse the process as in the case of the CAP. New members of the EC have suffered particularly from having to accept the *acquis communautaire*. They often had little say in the policy's formulation and yet find it contrary to national interests without any noticeable compensation elsewhere. A good example of this is the UK's conflict over the EC's budget – at least from the UK's point of view.

2.5 The EC budget

If a decision-making mechanism is to work, it must prove itself capable of resolving conflict. Within the EC, one of the longest running conflicts is the issue of the budget. Relative to the total national economies of the Community it looks relatively small. It amounted to 0.9 per cent of gross national product (GNP) and 2.8 per cent of public spending in 1983. It is significant in that firstly, it touches on many of the EC's policy areas. Secondly, the budget is an area where it is possible to identify tangible gains and losses. Finally, the budget is growing in size relative to the economies of member states, and it could be argued that this is essential if the EC is to develop.

Although the EC is unusual compared to most other inter-national organisations, in that it has a budget which provides funds for areas other than basic administration, it is still not like that of national economies because of the following reasons:

1. It has no macro-economic stabilisation role – its small size would preclude this in any case.
2. It cannot finance its activities by borrowing except in specific circumstances. The budget must therefore balance; there can be no deficit financing.
3. Spending areas are subject to separate sets of operating rules and are seen as being independent of one another.

Income

From 1958 to 1970 the EC was financed by contributions from member states, which although they were politically determined, were broadly based on ability to pay. Since 1970 the EC has operated on a system of 'own resources'; that is, income which it regards as its own as of right. It is made up of the following:

Customs duties
All duties that are collected by national customs officers automatically go to the EC. This is known as the Common Customs Tariff (CCT). The argument is that the goods could be destined for any

country within the EC, and therefore the duty amounts to a genuine shared income (see Ch. 3).

Agriculture and sugar levies
Agriculture levies are taxes on food imports used to keep out cheap imports from EC markets and thereby maintain the income of farmers. Sugar levies are charges on producers which are used to help to dispose of excess quantities. It also applies to producers of a sugar substitute, isoglucose.

Value added tax
From 1970 to the end of 1985 the ceiling on contributions was the product of up to 1 per cent of the value added tax (VAT) base. This ceiling was raised to 1.4 per cent as a result of the Fontaine-bleau Summit in 1984. The EC should not automatically collect the full 1.4 per cent, the percentage depends on the level of expenditure agreed. In practice the effect of the UK's budget abatement reduces the maximum average contribution of all member states to about 1.25 per cent of the VAT base. Because of Zero rated or certain exempt goods from VAT in countries like the UK, the actual payments are done on a standardised basis so you cannot reduce the contribution by reducing the VAT rate.

As expenditure has risen, the EC has had to rely increasingly on VAT payments as a source of income, as Table 2.1 illustrates. The reason for this, is the decreasing importance of customs duties, as tariff rates have fallen and trade has grown more rapidly between

Table 2.1 Growth in Community spending

Year	% increase in expenditure over previous year	% change in VAT revenue over previous year (EC Nine)	VAT % rate	% increase in farm guarantee spending over previous year
1979	13.7	9.1	0.78	20
1980	13.5	9.5	0.73	9
1981	12.0	17.9	0.79	−3
1982	15.8	11.1	0.92	12*
1983	19.8	5.7	1.00	14
1984	9.7	4.8	1.00†	30
1985	4.5	5.9	1.00†	9

Source: Commission of the EC. Quoted in *The Guardian*, 4 December 1986
* Greece now included.
† Some spending financed by advances. Without this, rate would be 1.13%.

17

Community partners. At the same time expenditure has grown in a number of policy areas.

Expenditure

Over the years, the EC expenditure programme has expanded, notably with the introduction of the European Regional Development Fund (ERDF) and the European Social Fund (ESF). In 1986 agricultural spending was due to take 66 per cent of total spending, compared to only 14 per cent for ERDF and ESF. The failure to achieve some kind of equitable redistribution mechanism led to an inevitable demand for direct reimbursement, which has been the source of fierce negotiation in recent years.

The budgetary process

The expenditure side of the budget is divided into two categories, which although they are not mentioned in the Treaty of Rome, are of considerable importance. They are:

1. *Compulsory expenditure* – this is regarded as obligatory expenditure in that the programmes are laid down in the Treaties, for example most of CAP spending.
2. *Non-compulsory expenditure* – this includes the ERDF and ESF plus most new items of expenditure.

The importance of the distinction is because of the degree of control that the European Parliament has over them.

The procedure for adopting the budget can be broken down into four stages following the approximate timetable indicated below.

Stage 1   Estimates are prepared and discussed by the Council of Ministers. By the end of July, the draft budget is agreed and forwarded to Parliament.

Stage 2   Parliament considers the draft budget by the end of October. It can only propose modifications to compulsory expenditure by a majority of members.

Stage 3   The draft budget is returned to the Council of Ministers, which meets again in December. Decisions made by the Council of Ministers on compulsory expenditure are final, but they have to decide to accept or reject any changes in non-compulsory spending.

Stage 4   The draft budget returns to the Parliament who have the final word on non-compulsory spending. The actual sum total of spending in this area is, however, limited by agreement. The Parliament then has the right to reject or accept the draft budget.

The power to reject or amend the draft budget gives the Parliament more power in the area than elsewhere. Despite this, the driving force is still the Council of Ministers. The failure to adopt a budget in time does not grind the EC to a halt. Expenditure is limited by the provisional 'twelfths regime'. This is where expenditure cannot exceed one-twelfth of the lower provision of the draft budget. This final point is a matter of dispute: it has been suggested that it can also be one-twelfth of the previous year's level of expenditure.

Budgetary conflict

In general, the area of the budget is always likely to generate conflict, if only because of the changing and evolving nature of the Community. Disputes over the budget go deeper than this, however, with a fundamental feeling of dissatisfaction with the equity of the budget by the UK which has continued since the first expansion in 1973. Without an acceptable balance between gains and losses a political system such as the EC is unlikely to be stable. Other problems have impinged upon the dispute, including the cost of the CAP and the way it crowds out other expenditure. Also, by the early 1980s, there was a realisation that the EC was simply going to run out of money without an increase in 'own resources'.

The origins of the UK's budgetary dispute

It was unfortunate that the EC adopted its system of 'own resources' before UK membership because it always looked as though the UK would be disadvantaged. On the revenue side, the UK's trade patterns meant more imports of manufactures and food came from outside the EC and were, therefore, subject to a greater incidence of payment of duty. On the expenditure side the smallness of the UK's agricultural sector meant that benefits in this area would be limited. Prior to the UK's accession the problem was recognised and it was agreed that if the burden became unacceptable, a solution would have to be found. When the Labour Government came to power, budgetary contributions were part of the renegotiation package. The solution that was agreed was largely cosmetic, and its terms were so onerous that little benefit was likely to result. It was based on economic indicators, which improved as a result of North Sea oil. The UK balance of payments moved into surplus and the pound revalued, which caused an apparent improvement in the UK's gross domestic product (GDP) per head from 75 per cent of Community average in 1978 to 98 per cent in 1981.

A second round of negotiation of the budget issue started in 1978, and this was taken up by the Thatcher Government in 1979. The failure of the 1975 mechanism led the UK to campaign for more than just a cosmetic solution to the problem of contributions. Along with this the UK campaigned for a changed balance of expenditure and some constraint on its total level.

After protracted negotiation an agreement was reached which lasted from 1980 to the end of 1983. The UK was refunded two-thirds of its unadjusted net contributions. This meant that instead of paying European Currency Units (ECUs) 6,868 million in total over the period the UK was to be refunded ECU 4,490 million, making a net contribution of ECU 2,378 million. Also, as part of the deal, there was to be more spending which would benefit the UK. Generally, Community institutions tend to favour a more expenditure-side solution, because they help to promote greater integration. This was not generous considering the UK's relatively poor position in the league table of incomes per head. Indeed it looked considerably worse in this respect, if we take C N Morris's

Table 2.2 Estimated resource cost of UK membership 1983 (ECU million)

Resource costs		Absolute gains	
VAT contribution	2,908	Higher prices paid to farmers	3,679
Customs duties	1,910	CAP	560
Higher prices paid to consumers	7,145	Regional funds	656
Net costs	11,963	Social funds	437
		Other resources and receipts	347
		Net gains	5,679

Resource cost ECU 6,284 million (net cost minus net gains). This compares with an estimated budgetary cost of ECU 1,966 million for UK membership.

Source: C N Morris 1984 *Future financing of the Community*, Report of the House of Lords Select Committee, pp 123–4

point that the EC's budget does not reflect the resource cost of membership. His calculations in Table 2.2 exclude the cost of maintaining higher agricultural prices, but consumer losses and 'producer gains' are included.

The budgetary process in this period was carried through with considerable rancour. In 1982, for example, attempts by the UK to hold up the farm price review to try to win further concessions on the budget resulted in the 'Luxembourg Compromise' being abandoned. The use of majority voting was regarded as a betrayal by the UK, although it did not herald a new era of decision making.

The Fontainebleau Agreement

The movement towards a more permanent settlement started to become more urgent as the VAT elements of 'own resources' started to become insufficient for the Community's commitments. In 1984 the Fontainebleau Summit established a solution to the budgetary problem as part of a package of measures. The UK won agreement for a refund of ECU 1,000 million for that year. In future years there was to be an automatic repayment of 66 per cent of the difference between the UK's VAT payments to the Community and its share of Community expenditure. The cash value of this rebate will rise as it was agreed that the VAT rate would be increased from 1 per cent to 1.4 per cent in 1986. It still leaves the UK as a net contributor, and as VAT and agricultural levies are excluded, the net contribution is reduced by half.

The agreement also suggested that there might be a possible rise of the VAT contribution to 1.6 per cent in 1988, although this was not a firm agreement. The Germans were also allowed to increase subsidies to their farmers. The new higher rate of VAT contributions was considered essential because of the cost of:

1. The CAP.
2. New policy areas.
3. Membership of Spain and Portugal which was calculated to cost between 0.1 and 0.2 per cent of VAT. (This may well be an underestimate if they succeed in developing EC policies fully.)

However, the Fontainebleau Agreement did not provide for a long-term solution to the EC's budget difficulties. The real value of the increase in resources was probably not more than the product of 0.15 per cent in the VAT element of 'own resources' because money was set aside for expansion, the UK rebate and for Greece as part of the Integrated Mediterranean Programmes. Almost as soon as the new VAT ceiling came into force it was swallowed up by increased agricultural spending, and by 1987 the budget faced a major crisis.

Lessons of the budget dispute

Over the years, budgetary contributions caused bitter disputes between the member states, and illustrates well the very nationalistic basis of EC bargaining and decision making. The UK's problem was not resolved until there was a genuine coincidence of need. The UK's agreement to increase the VAT rate was essential for the EC to continue to develop.

The UK accepted the existing budgetary system when she joined the EC, and it could be argued that it was not the EC's fault if the benefits of membership failed to compensate for the cost. Possibly the UK could have gained more if she had been prepared actively to support an expansion of Community programmes. The counter to this is that the budget rules were so biased that the UK, at that time one of the poorest members, was contributing 0.5 per cent of GNP in net terms to the Community. It may well be that on a culmulative basis this kind of an amount will affect economic performance. In any case, this kind of expenditure is politically difficult to justify in a period of economic stagnation. The UK's stance may be regarded as the pursuit of cynical self-interest, but other nations could equally well have the same charge levelled at them. The defence of the budgetary status quo, by the French for example, was clearly even more unreasonable when the incomes per head of the two countries are compared.

As Table 2.3 shows, the UK is still a net contributor to the budget, although perhaps, this is likely to be less contentious given the need for some transfer of resources to Spain and Portugal. There are some members who could afford to pay more, however, if the EC is to achieve an equitable solution to the budget. The position of Spain and Portugal will be considered in Chapter 10.

It is difficult to construct Community legislation so that some country is not disadvantaged. Disputes of this nature are likely to arise again therefore, especially as the EC is in constant danger of running out of money. Any new solution to the problem of budgetary contributions will almost certainly change the distribution of budgetary gains and losses. The fact that there are now 12 members involved in the decision process means that it is going to

Table 2.3 Winners and losers from the EC budget 1985

Country	% contributions to EC own resources	% of payments to member states
Belgium	5.0	4.3
Denmark	2.4	3.7
France	20.4	21.9
West Germany	28.8	17.0
Greece	1.5	6.9
Ireland	1.1	6.3
Italy	13.9	18.1
Luxembourg	0.2	0.0
Netherlands	7.2	9.0
UK	19.5	12.6
Allocation not available	0.2	

Source: EC Court of Auditors Report 1986

be even more difficult to resolve conflict. Majority voting is not the solution, nor can the European Parliament play a significant role, as essential national interests are involved. What is required is a genuine recognition that national interests are important and that there must be a reasonable balance of advantage to all. In particular, it seems always likely to be the case that those countries which contribute the most in terms of resources are always going to want the greatest influence on decision making.

Chapter three
Economic integration within the European Community

Economic integration means, within the context of the EC, the combining of the economies of the member states to form a much larger European economy. The purpose of the exercise is first to achieve an improvement in the economic welfare of the members. Secondly, it is hoped that this process will also promote political integration. In the absence of free trade, the degree of economic integration will depend, in part, on the political will of like-minded states to form agreements. Some of the possible types of agreements are listed below in order of the degree of commitment they require from participants.

1. Trade agreements
These give specific trade preference to certain countries. They may in some cases have a political motive, or be simply designed to assist in trade links.

2. Free trade areas (FTAS)
These are agreements to remove tariffs and quotas and some other restrictions which stop the flow of goods between members. The UK was a member of such an organisation called the European Free Trade Area (EFTA) from 1960 to 1973, designed to promote trade mainly in industrial goods. An FTA is a tariff-free area, but individual members may be free to set their own tariff levels against non-member states. In order to avoid trade being deflected via the country with the lowest tariff wall, rules of origin have to be used. Rules of origin should clarify where a product is manufactured for customs purposes, although definitions can be complex where components are purchased from outside the FTA, to be used in products assembled within it.

3. Customs unions

Customs unions have been used in the past to promote political as well as economic integration. The best-known example was the *Zollverein*, which was established in 1833, and contributed greatly towards the unification of Germany. The main features of a customs union are:

(a) Tariff barriers are eliminated between member states.
(b) A Common External Tariff (CET) is established. Within the EC, this is known as the CCT. This ensures that import duties are charged at the same rate regardless of the point of entry.
(c) The customs revenues are distributed among the members according to an agreed formula.

Features (b) and (c) help to overcome some of the problems of trade deflection.

4. Common markets

This is a further step along the road towards greater economic integration. It incorporates the existence of a customs union with features such as free movement of capital and labour. The harmonisation of business laws and some agreement as to non-tariff barriers is required. Finally, there should be common policies to deal with areas such as transport, energy, industry and taxation.

5. Economic union

This implies a complete abolition of differences in economic policy based upon the individual nation state. The economies of the economic union should be managed collectively as if the organisation is a completely integrated economic unit. In an economic union, there must inevitably be a considerable loss of economic sovereignty, so for example there would be just one currency with one central bank, and the basis of fiscal and monetary policy would have to be fully agreed. It is difficult to imagine this stage being reached without there being a high degree of political integration.

3.1 Trade and protection

For the economist, the ideal state of affairs is often where free trade exists, that is, where there are no man-made obstacles to the trade between nations. This is because free trade allows individuals to exploit their comparative advantage, and therefore specialise in what they do best. It leaves the consumer with a wider choice of goods at competitive prices. Within nation states, arguments to restrict trade between one area and another would be regarded as illogical. However, states see it as being in their interest to restrict international trade, in the hope that they will gain at the expense of others.

In good times, pressures to protect an economy may not be great, because if industries decline there are alternative sources of employment available for those whose jobs are displaced by imports. However, even when things are going well, sectional interests may be able to launch an effective campaign for exceptional treatment based upon pleas that the national interest could be served by protecting a particular industry. The immobility of labour may lead to substantial pockets of high unemployment for example. It is also frequently argued that temporary protection is required for certain industries, when they are either trying to become established, or when they face a period of change.

At times of high unemployment, cheap imports are often regarded as the cause of the national malaise, and so wider restrictions may be placed upon trade. Import protection has the benefit of being highly visible to the protected groups, and being off-budget. The consumer will have to pay higher prices for the goods he buys, but the effects are diffuse and difficult to calculate. There is of course, the risk of retaliation by states who feel that they have been treated unreasonably. The costs of retaliation are unlikely to be borne by the protected industries, but it may lead to those industries affected by it to call for help. If protection develops on a world-wide basis, then the multilateral trade system is likely to break down, and all countries will lose. This was the case in the 1920s and 1930s, when the world-wide recession was made considerably worse by countries attempting to maintain exports at the same time as reducing their dependence on imports. Eventually trade relations deteriorated to the point where the multilateral system of trade collapsed, and bilateral trade became the norm. That is, each trading country restricted access to its markets to those countries which offered specific trade concessions in return.

The theory of customs unions

The idea of a customs union is to create an area of free trade, so that once goods enter into it, or if they are produced within it, they are free to circulate without paying tariffs. Because goods may enter the union at any point, there are problems of distributing tariff receipts. The Netherlands, for example, receives a significant amount of cargo destined for West Germany, and if they were allowed to keep the tariffs for their own use, they would benefit at the expense of the Germans. To overcome this problem the EC uses all customs receipts to finance its activities. Imports into the customs union pay the same level of tariff regardless of the point of entry. Because of this tariff, the customs union discriminates in favour of member states, and against non-members. The degree of discrimination varies depending on individual trade agreements that the customs union has with external trading partners. The EC allows more generous terms to less developed countries than to Japan for example.

Initially, economic theory was kind to customs unions, as they were regarded as a step towards free trade. Jacob Viner, however, suggested that they may not always increase economic welfare if trade diversion is greater than trade creation. Trade diversion is the switching of supply of a particular good from a cheaper source outside the customs union to a more expensive one within it. An example would be agricultural products. The UK, prior to membership of the EC, was able to buy food at the cheapest prices on the world market, which was a significant benefit to a country which was a major food importer. As a result of EC membership the price of imported food rose significantly. Trade creation, on the other hand, is said to be a benefit in that it indicates that comparative advantages are being exploited, and that the consumer has a greater choice of products at more competitive prices.

It is possible to illustrate the phenomenon of trade creation by using a simple numerical example. In Table 3.1, A is the home country, B joins with A in the customs union and C is meant to represent the rest of the world. The product is cassette decks.

Table 3.1 Trade creation

Country	Price in £ before the customs union			Price in £ after the customs union		
	A	B	C	A	B	C
Cost of production	80	70	50	80	70	50
100% tariff imposed by A		70	50			50
Price in A	80	140	100	80	70	100

The European Community

Before the customs union is formed, A's consumers buy their cassette decks from home suppliers at £80 each, because of the effects of a 100 per cent tariff. Once the union is formed, it is possible for A's consumers to buy their cassette decks at £70 each from B. As a result of customs union, membership trade is being created. It is interesting to note that if the tariff levels had been different, it might change the benefits of membership. If the tariff is set at 50 per cent, A's consumers would be purchasing their decks from C, because they would cost only £75. Joining the union would be trade diverting, because purchases would shift to B as a more expensive source.

The trade effects of forming a customs union are illustrated in Fig. 3.1. Before the customs union came into existence, the country imposed a tariff which took prices up from P_1 P_3. This meant that consumer demand was less than it might have been at q_3.

If a customs union is formed with the partner country, supplies can be bought at P_2, so that home production will fall from q_2 to q_1, but consumption will increase from q_3 to q_4. Because of the effects of the common external tariff, existing purchases from the rest of the world would cease. The model therefore contains a mixture of trade creation and trade diversion as follows:

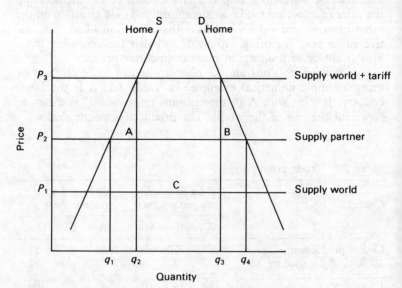

Fig. 3.1 The trade effects of forming a customs union

- A is the production effect, in that it represents the saving by importing q_1 to q_2.
- B is the consumption effect, that is, the savings made by the consumer, who now consumes q_3 to q_4 at lower prices.
- A and B are therefore the production and consumption effects of trade creation.
- C is the adverse effect of trade diversion, which is the increase in the price of imports from P_1 to P_2 multiplied by the quantity of imports q_2 to q_3.

There have been many criticisms of the above analysis, not the least from those who suggest that customs unions can only be a second-best solution. If trade creation is such a good thing, they argue, then why not go all the way and have free trade which gives no trade diversion? Even if trade diversion helps the exporter of higher priced goods, he is still an inefficient producer. While this argument holds true if all countries adopt free trade, this is not a practical suggestion. If a country moves towards free trade on a unilateral basis, there is no reason to think that others will follow. The advantage of forming a customs union is that it is one way of ensuring that those who participate will have certain tariff-free access to markets. Concessions are negotiated among a number of trading nations, and the union usually covers a wide range of products, so that for the union to work, there must be a general compliance with its rules.

The dynamic effects of customs union membership

So far we have looked at the static effect of joining a customs union. This is a once-and-for-all gain or loss, and does not take account of the influence that the union might have on the economies who are members. It would be surprising if membership of an organisation the size of the EC did not have long-term influence on the economic development of those within it, and indeed those states who remained outside. When the UK was preparing to join the EC, the static effect of membership was thought to be negligible, but the potential dynamic effects were said to be important. In particular, the opportunities for greater economies of scale, increased specialisation, the benefits of competition and the association with fast-growing economies were stressed.

Some of these benefits are difficult to measure, and may only be apparent in the long term. An example might be the argument that a competitive environment helps economies to develop. This suggests that the presence of competition helps to get rid of inefficiency within business, and acts like a 'cold shower', stimulating industry to modernise and improve. It could also reasonably be pointed out that competition can kill off whole sectors of industry which deserve to survive for the social good. In fact, there is little that can be proved in these kinds of debate, which is why they are popular with politicians who like to use them in order to rationalise political decisions.

A more promising area of investigation is the impact of economies of scale. N Owen[1] in his study of trade in industrial goods within the EC from the 1960s onward, regards competition between companies as being something of a brawl. There are many companies trading in very similar products within a mass market, and no one company can hope to produce the total range of products within a sector. Cost advantages are important, even though it may be the quality of the product that determines the success of sales in foreign markets. This is because the better the rate of profit, the more scope the firm has to develop non-price features.

Within a larger market, companies have the opportunity to increase production and enjoy falling costs. Some of these opportunities exist at the expense of other, less efficient, producers. This is illustrated in Fig. 3.2. In this example, variable costs such as wages and raw materials are the same for everyone, but fixed costs per unit of output fall with increased scale of production.

In the above case, we have three countries, A, B and C. If C's market is opened up to competition, as a result of joining a customs union with A and B, then the lowest-cost producer A can step into C's market. A's industry can as a result expand production from 200 to 300 units, and so further reduce its costs. C's industry is no longer able to compete, and so must go out of business, as prices fall to the level of the next most efficient producer B. As a result of falling prices, it is possible to envisage an increase in the overall size of the market, and if this process continues, progress can be made towards the optimum size of plant. This increased specialisation may not be well regarded by C, who experiences the inevitable loss of jobs.

If we take the production of refrigerators as an example of this process, we can see how the Italians were able to grow and dominate the market within the EC from having a very small-scale industry in the 1950s. By exploiting economies of scale, Italian producers were able to cash in on the expanding market for cheap family-sized refrigerators in the 1960s. By 1967 the average size of plant of those producers making up 50 per cent of each country's

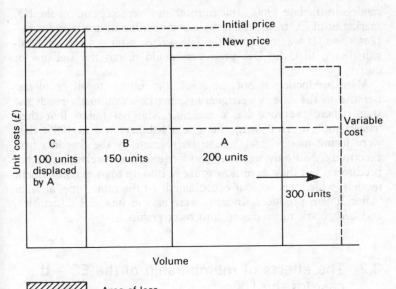

Fig. 3.2 Economies of scale and competition
Source: Adapted from Owen 1983

output varied considerably. In Italy, the most efficient country, the capacity of the largest producers averaged 850,000 units per year, compared to 570,000 for Germany, 290,000 for France and 170,000 for Britain.

By 1967, Ignis (later Philips) and Zanussi were producing 1 million and 700,000 units respectively. They relied on automated plants producing a narrow range of standardised volume refrigerators. The 'cheap and cheerful' product penetrated both the French and West German markets to such an extent that their competitors either went 'up market' or left the area of production. In some cases, firms imported Italian machines and resorted to vendor branding. Total Italian production rose from 500,000 units in 1958 to 5.4 million units in 1972.

Italian producers recognised early that the best probable size of plant to produce refrigerators with the level of technology available in the late 1960s and 1970s was one capable of producing about 800,000 units per year, while UK producers were thinking in terms of 200,000 units per year. As a consequence, Italian machines could be produced at something like 15 per cent less than similar UK models in the late 1960s. Italian machines were kept out of the UK market until EC membership by a combination of tariffs and transport costs. It was not until the late 1970s, after a series of amalgamations, that the UK producers could match the Italians for cost.

Mass production is not, however, the answer to all problems, because in the case of refrigerators, markets eventually reach the stage where everyone has a machine. Zanussi found that their 'cheap and cheerful' image became a liability, and in 1985, they were losing money, and had to be rescued by the Swedish firm Electrolux. Not only were they no longer efficient relative to other producers, but they were slow to move into up-market replacement models, which were colour coordinated. At the same time, another major Italian producer, Indesit, were also in financial difficulties, and had to ask to be placed into receivership.

3.2 The effects of membership of the EC – the case of the UK

When the UK joined the EC in 1973, she joined more than just a customs union. Although the common market had not been fully developed, a wide range of policies which affected the relationship between the nation state and the Community were in place. A problem arises when we try to separate these effects from other developments going on within the domestic and world economy. Major events like the the world recession and the increase in the size of the EC itself, make it difficult to decide what the outcome for the UK would be without membership.

The UK's economy has suffered from slow growth since joining the EC. In the first 11 years of membership, growth averaged only 1.5 per cent per year, compared to 2.7 per cent in the previous 11 years. However, economic growth in the whole of the EC fell from 4.5 to 2 per cent over the same period, which suggests that all economies have suffered from the same malaise. When the UK proposed membership in 1971, a White Paper suggested that membership might cause economic growth to increase by 0.5 per cent per year. Even this modest figure looks as though it has not been achieved. Johnson[2] for example, thinks that membership made a difference of 0.3 per cent per annum, or a cumulative 3.3 per cent after 11 years.

Perhaps the most important feature of the UK's economic

Table 3.2   United Kingdom trade with the EC (as a percentage – current membership throughout)

Year	Exports	Imports
1960	22	21
1970	30	27
1980	43	41
1983	44	46
1985	49	49

Source: Overseas trade statistics. Department of Trade

relationship with the EC is in the area of trade. The UK is a major trading nation, with about 30 per cent of its GDP being exported. As Table 3.2 shows, the percentage of UK imports and exports to and from EC countries has risen significantly since the EC's formation, and as a consequence the traditional dependence on Commonwealth trade has declined. In 1960 over 30 per cent of UK trade was with the Commonwealth, but this had declined to around 10 per cent by the mid 1980s.

Care should be taken with the interpretation of the above trends, because the Community has itself expanded. However, even before the UK joined, trade with the EC was increasing, although this may have been in anticipation of eventual membership. The switch of trade towards the Community was accompanied by a worsening trade balance, particularly in manufacturing, as is illustrated in Table 3.3.

Although the overall trade balance with the Community deterio-

Table 3.3   United Kingdom balance of trade with the EC

Year	Total trade balance (£B)	Export/import ratio (%)	Manufactures balance (£B)	Export/import ratio (%)
1970	+0.1	105	+0.6	143
1973	−1.3	76	−0.4	90
1979	−2.7	87	−2.6	83
1980	+0.8	104	−1.2	92
1983	−2.4	92	−7.2	69
1984	−3.1	91	−8.1	70
1985	−2.0	95	−8.7	72
1986	−8.3	81	−10.1	70

Source: Adapted from *Developments in the European Community* July–December 1986, pp 85, 86, HMSO Cm 122

rated in the early years of UK membership, things looked as though they were improving by 1980. This improving trend was partly due to oil sales to the Community, and perhaps the improving terms of trade the UK enjoyed due to the rise in the value of the pound. By 1982, the sale of oil could not mask the ever-increasing deficit in manufactures. The overvaluation of the pound meant that UK producers were unable to resist the flood of EC imports. The fall in oil prices in 1986 meant that the trade deficit with the Community widened dramatically in that year. The weakening value of the pound against the EMS currencies also worsened the trend, as imports became more expensive, and it took time for exporters to re-establish themselves in continental markets.

It was Europe's most efficient producer, West Germany, who was able to exploit the UK market most readily in manufacturing trade. Over 60 per cent of the manufacturing deficit was with West Germany, and the sector where the deficit was at its greatest was road vehicles. This was caused by price factors as well as doubtful reputation for quality. As the pound declined in value in the mid 1980s the major US multinational car producers realized the cost of transferring production out of the UK, and started to source the market by more domestic production. This meant that UK producers' share of the home market started to expand, but it takes a considerable amount of time to re-establish market share once it has been lost.

In general, UK business did not respond to the challenge of the EC at all well. This was partly due to a lack of preparation and strategic planning by UK companies. There is no doubt that some UK products could have sold well in EC markets, but a lack of information about the specific features of national and regional markets has hampered UK companies. However, the blame for any failures, cannot be placed entirely on the shoulder of UK producers. The overvaluation of the UK pound, and the fact that continental producers already enjoyed considerable economies of scale, meant that UK producers could be easily pushed aside. The assumption that British industry was fit and ready to compete was generally a false one.

3.3 Non-tariff barriers

So far we have assumed that it is tariff barriers that form the greatest obstacle to free trade. The Treaty of Rome, however, specifically required that not just the elimination of tariffs, but also the abolition of quantitative restrictions and other measures which have a similar effect. These non-tariff barriers were not thought to be of great importance, and in the first few years of its existence, the EC concentrated on the abolition of internal tariffs. Tariffs between member states were abolished on 1 July 1968, some 18 months ahead of schedule. This proved to be a relatively easy task, given the atmosphere of rapid economic growth, and the fact that with the exception of agricultural products, tariffs were relatively low. As tariffs were eliminated the extent of non-tariff barriers became apparent, and it was clear that they were a considerable obstacle to developing a genuine European economy.

The extent to which non-tariff barriers hamper trade is difficult to measure, because many of them are not apparent until there are complaints about them. They are, however, difficult to circumvent, because unlike tariffs, they cannot be overcome by a simple, if inconvenient, price reduction. For example the UK's prohibition on the importing of pasteurised milk on health grounds, guaranteed that the home market would be supplied exclusively by domestic producers. Usually non-tariff barriers are the result of government action, although in some cases business can be directly involved, as in the case of the trade in motor cars (see p. 37). Some of the barriers are of long standing, and were not designed specifically to hamper trade, for example, long-standing technical regulations. It is the case now that governments regulate so much of national economies, that they have direct control over a wide range of standards and trading practices, and this makes them a target for business and consumer groups. These groups are able to appeal to governments to regulate in their interest on the grounds of nationalism, tradition or economic threat. Since the early 1970s these groups have had increased success as the world recession, and the external threats from the newly industrialised countries (NICs) and Japan speed up the pace of deindustrialisation.

3.4 Reforming the internal market

In its ideal form the internal market should comprise an area without internal frontiers, in which the free movement of goods, persons, services and capital is ensured. Improving the workings of the internal market has been seen as an increasingly important policy priority in recent years. It is a cause which finds particular favour with those governments which believe that creating the right kind of competitive environment helps the process of economic growth. In particular, it is believed that a market free of national restrictions would:

1. Allow the full exploitation of the enlarged market of 320 million people.
2. Ensure that the market is expanding rather than being static.
3. Benefit the consumer, by offering a wider choice of goods at lower prices.
4. Speed up the process of political integration.

The process of improving the operation of the internal market depends on ensuring that the existing treaties are complied with, and that new legislation is passed in appropriate areas. There have been a number of important cases before the Court of Justice which have helped to establish free movement of goods. An interesting example is the challenge to the West German beer laws, which was resolved by the Court in 1987. The *Reinheitsgebot* is one of West Germany's most ancient laws dating back to a Bavarian edict of 1516, and it states that beer can only contain malt, hops and water. This meant that the whole range of chemical preservatives could not be used, and it had the effect of excluding most imported beers from the West German market, with the exception of products like Guinness. It also meant that West German beer did not travel well, and only 5 per cent of output was exported. As a consequence, West German breweries have remained as relatively small-scale affairs compared to those in the rest of the Community.

The Commission regarded the beer laws as a restriction on trade. However, despite the fact that most of the foreign preservatives used in beer are widely used in other West German products, the West Germans thought the exclusion of beer with added ingredients as a reasonable public health measure. The defence maintained that the sheer quantity of beer drunk, meant that the intake of chemicals would be unacceptably high. The average Bavarian drinks 235 litres per year, compared to 45 litres for the French, which seems to indicate that the real health problem lies with the Bavarians. Despite the Court ruling against them, most West German producers maintained that they intended to continue to produce the pure product; they may, however, change their views once significant quantities of cheap imported beers start to penetrate their supermarkets.

Not all non-tariff barriers to trade are maintained directly by member governments. The car market has suffered from considerable distortions in recent years, with very large differences in prices for the same models between member states. Up to the mid 1980s, it was possible to make savings of several hundreds of pounds by buying a car in Belgium and importing it into the UK. The VW Golf GTI, for example, cost £4,714 in Belgium, as against £6,315 in the UK in July 1984. It was estimated by the Institute of Fiscal Studies in 1982 that the cost to the UK consumers in higher prices was £1.3 billion, or 0.6 per cent of GDP, and the foreign exchange cost was about £650 million. The main beneficiaries were the car companies who were able to sustain the higher prices at the expense of the UK consumer. (Billion = One thousand million.)

Part of the reason for this extraordinary state of affairs was the overvaluation of sterling, which made UK producers particularly uncompetitive. In normal market conditions there would have been a flood of imports into the UK, and a consequent reduction of price. However, foreign producers were reluctant to cut prices, because they preferred increased profit margins and they did not want to upset domestic producers. They preferred to compete actively among each other on style and other non-price factors, while they gradually gained market shares at the expense of particularly British Leyland, the major domestic producer.

This kind of price discrimination between countries can only be maintained by either relying on consumer loyalty to home-based retailers, or by making it difficult to import cars except by official channels. The UK Government made it difficult to import large quantities of cars except by authorised dealers, and they only begrudgingly permitted personal imports. Added to this, car producers were reluctant to make right-hand-drive cars available on the Continent. This caused the Commission to remind the producers that they must make all models available, even if they are going to be exported into other markets by individuals.

In an attempt to overcome the problem of the price differentials, a new EC regulation came into effect in 1985. It is likely to be ineffective, however, since sanctions only apply if prices differ by an average of 12 per cent in any one year, or by 18 per cent at any particular time. Countries where there are high retail taxes or price controls are exempt. Despite the lack of effective action by the Community, many of the differences between the UK and Belgium simply disappeared in 1986, with the fall in the value of the pound. If any lesson is to be drawn from this, it is that monetary stability is an important element in creating a unified market.

In order to make progress with reform of the internal market, the Commission published some 300 proposals for reform in a White Paper in 1985, and called for their implementation by 1992.

These proposals were under three broad headings, which were:

1. The removal of physical barriers.
2. The removal of technical barriers.
3. The removal of fiscal barriers.

The proposals were largely well received, although the UK and West Germany did express doubts about fiscal harmonisation. The problem is, however, getting the proposals accepted on a detailed basis, especially since the use of the veto to defend 'vital' national interest is unlikely to be totally abandoned. The Single European Act strengthened the Commission's proposals by incorporating within the Treaty the 1992 deadline, and made provision for voting on measures by a qualified majority. The right of member states to protect themselves from the danger of trade in drugs, terrorism and illicit works of art was maintained.

The speed at which proposals for reform are accepted depends on the political will, and the resources being available. Up to September 1987 only 75 of the 190 proposals put to the Council of Ministers had been passed, despite a significant speeding up during the British Presidency. The problem of delay arises in part, from trying to find any political consensus for proposals, but it also became clear that a major series of reforms requires very considerable staff resources which were not available.

The removal of physical barriers

These physical barriers exist at the customs posts throughout the Community. These posts exist as a convenient point to check on the compliance of national rules with regard to indirect taxation. They are also useful for protection against the movement of terrorists, drugs and, for the UK, the movement of animals which might have rabies. Border controls are estimated to add between 2 and 10 per cent to the cost of goods as they move from one country to another. Much of the burden arises from the cost of documentation, and the delays at border crossings. It normally takes a lorry in excess of five hours to clear customs at Dover for example. Lorry drivers eventually reacted against delays, and in February 1984 they block-aded French and Italian motorways in protest. These delays, it is hoped, will be much reduced with the introduction of the Single Administrative Document (SAD) in 1988. This replaces the numerous documents required to move goods from one country to another. For travellers, the actual process of moving between coun-tries has been speeded up on a bilateral basis. The Benelux countries have had virtually open borders for a long time, and in 1984, travel between France and West Germany was eased with the introduction of green channels which motorists could drive through with the minimum of checks.

The removal of technical barriers

National health regulations and technical standards frequently restrict trade within the EC. They often mean that goods that are safe, and which can be legally sold in one country, are not allowed to enter another market, as is the case with beer imports into West Germany. In 1985, it was estimated that only about 170 technical standards had been set for the EC, a rate which was far slower than the abilities of national governments to generate them; indeed, it has taken on average 10 years to agree on each EC standard. The result is that Europe remains a fragmented market. If we take the example of the market for televisions for example, Philips produce over 100 different types of set to meet the differing European standards. France operates on the SECAM system, while the UK and West Germany use different versions of PAL. Once products are established, these standards are difficult to change, as the Commission found when they tried to harmonise the rules with regard to chocolate products. In the original Six, the term 'chocolate' can only be used to describe products where cocoa butter is the only fat used. In the UK, Denmark and Ireland, up to 5 per cent of other vegetable fats can be used, and therefore their products cannot be sold as chocolate in a wider market. Suggestions to overcome the problem either involved a change in UK recipes, relaxing the rules in the Six, or renaming the UK product 'vegolate', 'fat glazing' or 'cocoa fantasy'. It is easy to see why these solutions proved to be unacceptable.

Under the heading of 'technical barrier', the Commission dealt with the problem of public procurement. Public authorities purchases amount to something between 8 and 9 per cent of Community GDP, yet almost invariably, well over 90 per cent of contracts are placed with domestic suppliers. In some cases, foreign equipment is provided by domestic contractors, but the absence of competitive tendering means that the prices charged to governments is frequently well above those ruling in the open market.

Purchases made with the help of Community funds are required to be subject to open tendering. Since 1978, public supply contracts of over ECU 2 million are supposed to be advertised in the Communities' *Official Journal*. Public works contracts over

ECU 1 billion have also to be advertised. These tendering requirements are frequently circumvented by governments, either by splitting contracts, so that they appear to be worth less than the
required amounts, or by direct negotiation of contracts. Important
areas are excluded from the above requirements, for example telecommunications, and national governments prefer to keep it that
way, in order to promote home-based technology. This is despite
the duplication of development costs and market fragmentation
involved. The Commission believes that neither the spirit or the
letter of the existing directives is respected.

The lack of a common transport policy is also considered a technical barrier. Transport represents more than 7 per cent of the
Community's GDP, and yet is the subject of considerable inter-
ference by member states. The Community operates a system of
truck permits which are allocated to nations on a quota basis.
Those lorries with permits are allowed to ply their trade freely
throughout the Community, picking up and delivering loads where
they wish. EC permits covered only about 15 per cent of cross-
border traffic however, and most movements were subject to bilateral arrangements. In 1985 there were 5,268 permits, and in 1986
this was increased by 15 per cent, plus an allowance for Iberian
membership, taking the total up to 7,437 permits. In 1986 it was
agreed that permits should be increased by an annual compounded
rate of 40 per cent, so that the quotas which were designed to
protect national carriers will be phased out. They meant that
haulage costs tend to be far higher than is justified by cost, and
the Commission estimated that 30 per cent of trucks returned to
base empty.

It was only in 1986, that the first elements of a maritime policy
started to emerge. It was agreed that restrictions on all routes to
and from and between member states were to be lifted. Also,
bilateral route-sharing agreements with non-member countries were
to be removed. However, ships are still not free to ply for cargoes
in the coastal waters of other member states, so that once again,
a free market still does not exist.

The case of air passenger traffic, is a particular scandal. Typically, the rate per mile tends to be something like five times higher
on scheduled routes within Europe than that which applies to
charter flights or on transatlantic routes. In 1985 the fare from
London to Miami cost 5.74 pence per mile, and a charter fare from
London to Malaga cost 5.57 pence per mile. This contrasts with
the scheduled fare from London to Brussels at 38.8 pence per mile,
and the London to Rome fare at 23.87 pence per mile. The ruling

by the Court of Justice in April 1986 that price-fixing by airline cartels was, in principle, in breach of the EC's competition laws, means that eventually, there will be greater competition on EC routes. This does not mean that there is ever likely to be full deregulation in the style of the USA, because the member states still wish to defend the position of their flag-carrying airlines. It should, however, mean that the consumer should get a better deal in future.

The removal of fiscal barriers

In the White Paper, the Commission proposed that fiscal frontiers be removed, and that there should be 'approximation' of the structures and rates of indirect taxation. This was is order to ensure the smooth passage of goods across frontiers, and prevent distortions in production costs and selling prices which affected competition. Rates of VAT vary between zero at the bottom rate in the UK, to 38 per cent for the higher rate in Italy, while the excise duty on a litre of wine varies between nil in Germany and ECU 2.74 in Ireland. Large numbers of people now simply cross over borders on shopping sprees in order to take advantage of the price differentials that this lack of fiscal harmonisation causes. It has been estimated that the trade costs the Irish £300 million per year in lost sales and the Danes £270 million per year. In 1987, in order to stop the damage of the lost sales to their economies, both governments placed a ban on day shoppers bringing in large quantities of duty-paid goods. This was despite protests from the Commission that such measures contravened the EC's border traffic directive.

In order to remove the fiscal frontier for VAT, the Commission proposed that zero-rating of VAT should cease, and that importers could reclaim the tax they pay from their own government, rather than from the country from which the goods were exported at the border. This implies that a 'clearing-house' will need to be established, as without this the exporting countries will gain at the expense of importing countries. Goods attracting excise duties, such as spirits, should be able to transfer from the bonded warehouse in one country to one in another.

Approximation of indirect taxation implies that the rates should be roughly, but not exactly, the same in each member country. Drawing on the experience of the USA, the Commission suggests that there should be a permissible variation of no more than 5 per cent in VAT, so that member states can vary their rates by no more than $2\frac{1}{2}$ per cent either side of a Community norm. As a first step in the process, the Commission suggest that there should be a standstill, so that differences do not become greater.

3.5 The People's Europe

Reform of the Community should be of direct benefit to its citizens, and not be just a business-related thing. In 1984, following the Dublin European Council, a committee was set up with a membership consisting of the leaders' personal representatives. This committee, under the chairmanship of Pietro Adonnino[3], produced a series of suggestions in 1985. Many of these are not new, but they offer the hope of reforms that the citizen can identify with. They include:

1. Increasing adult travellers' tax paid allowances (i.e. the amount of goods that individuals can carry with them when they cross borders).
2. A more uniform electoral system for the European Parliament.
3. Setting up a European Ombudsman.
4. EC-model driving licences – not the same licence in each country, but if a licence is issued in one country, it should not require replacing if a citizen moves to another country.
5. Cross-border television, perhaps with a Euro TV channel.
6. Acceptance of education credits won in one country by institutions in another.

3.6 Conclusion

The EC has not yet achieved the status of being a common market. There are still so many restrictions on trade that reform of the internal market must be regarded as a priority. The speed of reform is, however, highly dependent on the decision-making process, and a general acceptance that the balance of reforms are an advantage to all member states. If sectional interests are allowed to delay the completion date of 1992, then the consumer will undoubtedly pay some of the cost. Added to this, the competitive position of Europe in relation to the rest of the world is likely to deteriorate. Finally, although the Adonnino Report covers wider aspects than just the internal market, it does set the reforms in context. The citizen is important, and must be seen to benefit directly, otherwise there will be no popular interest in these largely technical issues.

3.7 References

1. N Owen 1983 *Economies of Scale, Competitiveness, and Trade Patterns Within the European Community*. Oxford.
2. C Johnson 1984 Memorandum to the Treasury and Civil Service Sub-Committee in the Treasury and Civil Service Select Committee Report. *The Financial and Economic Consequences of UK Membership of the European Communities* (1985) 57–11. HMSO.
3. Pietro Adonnino 1985 Report from the *ad hoc* Committee on a *People's Europe Bulletin of the EC* No 3.

Chapter four

The Common Commercial Policy

The EC is a dynamic trading block whose economy represents approximately 15 per cent of world GDP. External trade is important to the EC; it amounted to 27 per cent of GDP in 1985, compared to under 8 per cent for the USA and just under 15 per cent for Japan. The importance of extra EC trade within the world economy is illustrated in Table 4.1. As a consequence of being the largest trading block, the EC is not only vulnerable to trends within the world economy, but it also helps to shape them.

As we saw in the last chapter, free trade should exist within the EC's customs union. Trade relations with non-members are governed by the Common Commercial Policy (CCP), the centrepiece of which is the CCT. The simple purpose of the CCP is to achieve uniform trading relations between the EC and non-members. Such policy should benefit the Community's trading position by:

1. Protecting the CCT.

Table 4.1 Shares of world trade 1984 (intra-Community trade not included)

	Imports (%)	*Export* (%)
Euro Twelve	22	21
USA	21	15
Japan	9	11
Canada	5	6
USSR	5	6
Rest	38	41
	100	100

Source: EUR 12 *European File* 1986

completed, the Dillon Round 1960–62, the Kennedy Round 1954–67 and the Tokyo Round 1973–79. They have reduced the level of tariffs among developed economies to very low levels. So although the Tokyo Round reduced tariffs by about 38 per cent, its impact is likely to be small. The weighted average tariff is likely to be 4.8 per cent for the EC, 4.4 per cent for the USA and 2.6 per cent for Japan.[1] Tariff reductions were nowhere near as generous for goods from developing countries, such as textiles where the tariff cut was only 2 per cent and shoes where the cut was 16 per cent.

The Tokyo Round resulted in some agreement with regard to agricultural trade, accepting the highly protectionist mechanism of the CAP. Also, a series of codes was adopted which should help to improve the position with regard to non-tariff barriers covering customs valuation, technical barriers to trade, government purchasing, subsidies and countervailing duties and measures to combat dumping. It was not compulsory for all GATT members to sign these codes, and it was also possible to exclude parts of the codes. Many developed economies exploited these loopholes, for example by excluding telecommunications equipment from the code concerned with government purchasing. The result was that domestic industry was protected, but the effectiveness of the codes was limited.

In 1986 a new round of trade liberalisation negotiations was launched, called the Uruguay Round. This aims to roll back some of the trade restrictions which have crept in over the last few years. It is also meant to take action in order to liberalise the trade in services and agriculture. Also included is the protection of intellectual property rights, for example patents and trade marks, and a reduction in the scope of VERs. voluntary export restraints

4.2 The EC and trade regulation

The CCT was designed to keep competitive pressures from outside the customs union under control. In normal circumstances, home producers of manufactures enjoy the advantage of market knowledge and low transport costs, so that the existence of the CCT should ensure that they retain a substantial share of domestic markets. For a variety of reasons, however, the CCT is supplemented by other methods of trade regulation. These include:

1. *Agricultural levies*. The EC wishes to ensure that domestic agricultural producers achieve stable prices for their products. For

this reason a variable levy on agricultural imports is employed, so that if world agricultural prices fall the levy increases and vice versa if they rise.

2. *Anti-dumping measures.* Dumping is the selling of products on the overseas market at lower prices than apply to the home market. This is a traditional way of boosting exports but can be damaging to producers in the importing country. In order to counteract this unfair competition anti-dumping duties can be imposed.

3. *Quantitative restrictions.* These limit the flow of imports into the Community or member state to a specific amount. They are used in situations where Community production is threatened by the export activities of low-cost producers. In recent years the use of VERs has become widespread, and it is a form of control which individual members states are particularly fond of using.

While attempting to reform the internal market, the EC and individual member states have erected a number of restrictions on products from outside the Community. Page estimates that the EC Nine increased the coverage of managed trade on all goods from 35.8 per cent in 1974 to 44.8 per cent in 1980.[2] The starting-point looks high because agricultural products are included. More disturbing, however, is the increase in the coverage of managed trade in manufacturing goods. This rose from 0.1 per cent in 1974 to 17.4 per cent in 1980. This is no worse than the situation apparent in the rest of the trading world, but does show a growing protectionist trend.

The use of restrictions has increased as a result of a slowing down of the world economy. The EC's economic performance has also been deteriorating relative to the world's most successful exporting countries. In particular, vulnerable industries have led the cry for relief from aggressive exporters. Governments in turn have been unwilling to pay the budgetary cost of intervention and have sought to pass the costs of protection on to the citizens. The EC has at times been prepared to impose restrictions in addition to those applied by member states; although the use of these generally falls within the rules of the GATT it does not adhere to their intention.

For this reason, Community trade restrictions do tend to create trade disputes, although only major economic entities can offer a real challenge to the EC. The externalising of conflicts has the advantage for the EC of replacing internal enmities and can therefore help promote integration, but at the expense of consumers.

4.3 Operating the CCP

While the EC appears no more protectionist than other trading entities, the CCP is regarded by its critics as confusing and inefficient. Part of its problems arise from the lack of harmonisation of the import and export regulations which are applied by different member states. Although the CCT is fixed on a Community-wide basis, the processing through customs posts can vary considerably between states. A spectacular example of this came in 1982 when the French customs insisted that all Japanese videotape recorders should be diverted through the small customs post of Poitiers. This caused massive delays, not apparent in other states. These difficulties were caused by the reluctance of members to surrender further control to the Community. This split in responsibility for trade policy limits the authority of the Commission in its negotiations with non-member states. It hampers the process of harmonisation and gives rise to the need for rules of origin within the Community. As national governments impose 'voluntary' marker shares on their own account, these must be policed. In the case of the UK for example, the Japanese have agreed to limit their car exports so that they take no more than 11 per cent of the market.

For goods to be of EC origin they must be predominately made within the Community. Usually this is determined by value added. In the case of electrical goods it is 45 per cent, but for cars it is much higher at 60 per cent. These rules can cause problems for joint ventures involving non-EC companies. British Leyland, for example, had a great deal of difficulty selling the Triumph Acclaim in Italy, because it was the result of collaboration with Honda. Initially the Acclaim was regarded as being subject to a 3,000 limit for Japanese cars into that market. However, this decision was reversed.

4.4 The economic effect of Voluntary Export Restraint VER

The term 'voluntary' is of course misleading; these are agreements to restrict exports, which are a substitute for perhaps more severe compulsory controls. Within the Community, VERs are widespread. They tend to apply on a bilateral basis between member states and specific countries. For example, the UK requires that exports of footwear from Taiwan, colour TVs from Japan and

Christmas cards from the USSR are restricted. These restrictions are usually for an agreed period of time, and are actually administrated by the exporting country. On a Community basis, VERs have been applied to Japanese videotape recorders. Developing countries are also affected by the VER imposed under the Multi-Fibre Arrangements (MFA). These were introduced in order to protect EC producers from competition by low-labour-cost countries. Finally, some VERs are imposed on a unilateral basis because producers fear that action might be taken against them. In December 1985, the Japanese Ministry of International Trade and Industry announced they would be monitoring the volume of their exports of videotape recorders, colour TV sets and tubes, cars, commercial vehicles, fork-lift trucks and machining centres. The motive was clearly to ensure that excessive export volumes did not invite retaliation.

The use of VERs has encouraged the Japanese in particular to set up production plants within the EC. They offer the exporter the chance to avoid imposed controls and have negotiations as to the level of exports. The exporter may also receive a higher price for his goods than if a tariff was imposed. In Fig. 4.1 below, we see the effect of VERs.

In the above case, if only home supplies are available, the price will be P_3 and the quantity demanded will be OQ_3. If, however, world supplies are allowed into the market, prices will fall to P_1 and the quantity demanded will expand to OQ_5. The share of the

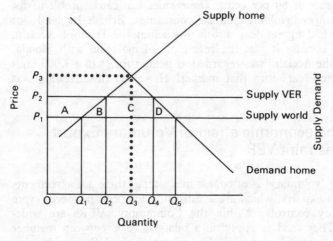

Fig. 4.1

market available to home suppliers will then contract to OQ_1. This may not be satisfactory, because it means that the industry has to contract, creating political pressures. In order for the industry to retain a larger share of the market OQ_2, a VER is imposed. This means that prices rise to P_2, and foreign supplies have to be content with only Q_2Q_4 of the market. Consumers will now find themselves paying higher prices, and will lose to the extent of ABCD. Area A will be a transfer from home consumers to home producers, who will now receive a higher price for their product. Area B is a dead-weight loss, because less efficient producers are supplying the market. Area D is a loss, because home consumers will now consume less. However, area C is the most significant loss because this is the gain to overseas suppliers who now receive a higher price at the expense of home consumers. This can offer exporters a considerable bonus, for example it is estimated that such gains may be worth about 1 per cent of Hong Kong's GNP. The extent to which an economy can gain does of course depend on the size of its market share.

The cost of trade restrictions to the Community was estimated to be in excess of £80 billion per year.[3] In terms of individual items, it probably adds 15 per cent to the price of Japanese cars and 15–25 per cent to the price of textiles and clothing from Hong Kong.[4] If indeed protectionism is desirable, the use of VERs would seem most inappropriate. It is far better to use tariffs, which at least may yield an income which can be used for other purposes.

4.5 The structure of EC trade

Table 4.2 shows the structure of the EC's trading relations. It illustrates the extent to which Community trade is concerned with the developed world. Within this group, intra-Community trade predominates, followed by trade within Western Europe. The USA is next in order of importance, followed by Japan, although the imbalance between imports and exports with Japan is a particular problem.

4.6 The European Free Trade Area

This is a free trade area consisting of six countries – Austria, Iceland, Norway, Sweden, Switzerland and, most recently, Finland who joined at the end of 1985. The total population of EFTA

Table 4.2 The Community of Ten's main trading partners
1958–85

| | *Imports* (%) | | *Exports* (%) | |
	1958	*1985*	*1958*	*1985*
Intra EC	34.0	51.6	34.9	52.5
Extra EC	66.0	48.4	65.1	47.5
Extra EC by area				
Other European OECD	18.2	27.5	25.1	29.6
USA	17.3	16.0	12.0	21.3
Canada	5.7	1.8	3.4	2.5
Japan	1.1	6.8	1.0	2.5
Australia	4.1	1.3	3.8	1.9
OPEC	16.5	19.0	12.0	19.0
Developing countries	29.5	15.8	31.0	13.2
Centrally planned	5.3	9.2	5.9	7.8
Rest of world	2.3	2.6	5.8	2.2
Total	100.00	100.00	100.00	100.00

Source: Adapted from the *European Economy*, No. 29, July 1986, p 159

members is only 32 million. However, income per head at the end of 1985 was $11,322 compared to $8,060 for the EC Ten and $6,684 for the EC Twelve (where reference to $ is made this indicates US dollars). It was established in 1960 as a counter to the EC with the UK as its most dominant member. Although concerned mainly with trade in industrial goods, some manufactured agricultural products and fishery products are covered by its activities. When the UK departed from EFTA in 1973 to join the EC, along with Ireland and Denmark, a free trade agreement was signed between the remaining EFTA countries and the EC, and import duties were abolished on most industrial goods in July 1977. The process with regard to industrial goods was completed as a result of the EFTA–EC trade meeting in April 1984. The EFTA countries do not wish for the political aspects of European integration; however, their joining with the EC in a widened free trade area of 352 million people does increase the bargaining power of the EC.

Although free trade exists among EFTA members, tariff levels against non-members vary from state to state. This means that elaborate rules of origin are required for intra-EFTA trade, to ensure that imports are not deflected via the lowest tariff point. Intra-EFTA trade is, however, relatively unimportant compared to trade with the Community. In 1985, 58 per cent of imports came from the EC and 52.8 per cent were exported there, making EFTA highly dependent on the Community. In most events concerned with trade EFTA generally tends to follow the EC's lead and accepts EC trade rules. They intend, for example, to introduce the SAD which is due to be brought into general use in the EC in 1988 (see Ch. 3), although with some seven boxes for extra information. This should ensure smooth passage of trade between the two. It would seem that the place of EFTA is likely to be firmly within the ambit of the EC, relying on its access to markets and seeing it as a haven in an increasing tripolar world dominated by the Japanese, the USA and the EC.

4.7 Japan and the EC

The Japanese economy has been more successful than that of the EC in recent years. Economic growth has tended to be an export-led phenomenon, with the Japanese being able to penetrate and displace the world's two other major trading entities, the USA and the EC. In 1984 the Japanese trade surplus was $35 billion, by 1985 this had grown to $49.3 billion and was expected to be in the region of $58 billion in 1986. The EC's trade deficit with Japan rose to $16.7 billion in 1986, up 3.5 per cent from 1985. This was despite about 40 per cent of Japanese imports into the Community being subject to some kind of protection mechanism.

Japanese export success has been achieved by producing high-quality goods at competitive prices. In general, there has also been a reluctance to move the yen's exchange rate upward to take account of surpluses, although continuing surpluses have made this inevitable. Their marketing efforts have been superior to those of many of their competitors and they have proved to be skilled trade negotiators. In particular, Japan has been able to exploit the trade rivalries within the EC, persuading members actively to compete with one another for direct investment, and thus Japan has avoided many of the potential consequences of concerted joint action against imports into the Community. To a certain extent, the EC tends to be hypocritical about the extent of the bilateral deficit, because the EC has in turn got a substantial trade surplus with the USA. If trade is to be multilateral, trade deficits should eventually balance each other out in the world trading system.

A continuing source of frustration for the EC is the lack of ability of Community-based firms to penetrate the Japanese market of 120 million people. Less than a quarter of Japanese imports are comprised of finished manufactures compared to 44 per cent for the EC and 52 per cent for the USA. This is explained by the Japanese as a function of a lack of selling effort of foreign firms, and a general need to import raw materials into a country with few natural resources. Over 500 European companies have been established in Japan in the last 10 years, showing that there is a market that can be penetrated. Despite the lack of firm controls over imports, however, many who try to sell to Japan find that the distribution network is inefficient, and that cultural attitudes are difficult to comprehend. Also, technical standards often make for very effective non-tariff barriers.

The final major area of concern for the Community is the Japanese ability to achieve great success in narrow sectors of production, particularly in areas like consumer durables, microelectronics and motor vehicles. This gives rise to difficulties in those sectors of the economies who face Japanese competitors. Despite the frequent introduction of trade restrictions, few countries have proved able to adapt to the flexibility and efficiency of Japanese producers.

The Japanese Government is clearly concerned with the threat of further protectionism, and has in recent years tried to encourage imports into the country, as well as controlling exports into sensitive markets. The Commission feels that more could be done to open up the Japanese market, and believes that despite much-publicised attempts at trade liberalisation the Japanese are still very protectionist. The attempt to introduce a new ski standard in 1986, to take account of the wet snow conditions that Japan is supposed to have, is an example of the way they use technical standards to protect their markets. In this case the standard had to be withdrawn because of international pressure. Substantial fiscal barriers are also in place, for example domestic whiskey producers enjoy a 792 per cent protection against EC imports. The Commission also feels that the Japanese are frequently slow to take the value of the yen upward, despite surpluses. Overall, therefore, much more needs to be done to move trade back towards a more respectable balance.

4.8 The United States and the EC

The EC and the USA between them represent some nine-tenths of the old industrial world. Both entities share many common values, particularly with respect to trade, although as we shall see there are areas of disagreement. The USA has a population of 238 million people with incomes per head about 40 per cent higher than those of the EC Twelve. The US and EC economies have tended to become increasingly interdependent, with events in one affecting the other. An example of this was the impact of high US interest rates, the value of the dollar and the US trade deficits of the mid 1980s. The USA enjoyed a balance of payments surplus of $6.3 billion in 1981, but the effect of an expanding domestic economy, and a massive rise in the value of the dollar, meant that in 1985 the annual trade deficit was $124.5 billion. It was estimated that $97.5 billion was due to a deteriorating trade in manufacturing goods. This deficit continued to worsen in 1986, to reach $170 billion for that year, despite a fall in the value of the dollar against most major currencies. The implications for the EC were that if the USA got rid of that deficit without the EC being able to gain in other markets, it would represent a substantial drain on Community balance of payments. In particular, it offered a threat to large exporters like West Germany, who had done particularly well out of that market.

The persistence of deficits meant that the protectionist spirit was strong in the USA. A major area of dispute in this respect was steel in the early 1980s. Throughout the world, steel producers faced crisis. In the EC, plant utilisation rates fell to less than 60 per cent. The EC responded to the crisis by a programme of restructuring at both national and Community level. The US steel producers also faced similar problems and needed to adjust capacity. They also faced a tide of imports which was difficult to stem. Imports penetration was about 13 per cent in 1976, it rose to 19 per cent in 1981 and 22 per cent in 1982. Under the threat of direct action in the form of punitive duties, the EC agreed to accept 'voluntary' restraint on its exports to the US market. These measures were insisted upon, in order to allow US industry to restructure itself. The Americans felt that restructuring measures within the EC amounted to unfair competition because they were financed by the member governments.

The longest-running trade dispute between the EC and USA has been in the area of agricultural sales. The USA has, with some reluctance, accepted the principle of Community preference and self-sufficiency within the EC. However, it finds attempts to unload the CAP's persistent surpluses onto the world markets at cut prices unacceptable. In 1981, US agricultural exports peaked at $44 billion, but by 1985 they had fallen to $31 billion. This faltering performance is partly related to the over-valuation of the dollar, but as the currency weakened, so exports became more competitive. This, combined with an aggressive trade strategy, has made EC farm exports increasingly expensive to subsidise.

In 1986 attempts were made to bring the CAP into effect in Spain and Portugal. First the Commission introduced a variable levy for maize imports into Spain so doubling the cost of selling US maize into the market. Second, the Portuguese cereals market, which was formerly the domain of US suppliers, was restricted by reserving 15.5 per cent of it for EC suppliers. Finally, quotas were put onto oil-seed imports, so limiting soya-bean sales. The trade losses were estimated to be $120 million, with a total potential trade loss of $600 million. While there will be some advantages to non-members from the freeing of these markets in industrial goods, with lower tariffs, there is no certainty that this will directly benefit the USA. In any case, it is no compensation for US farmers.

In the earlier expansions of the Community, the USA was prepared to accept fairly modest compensation for being excluded from EC markets. This was because of their support for the political aims of the EC. While still retaining some enthusiasm for European integration, the huge trade gap of the mid 1980s, plus declining farm sales, made this kind of action less acceptable. The USA felt that talks should have been held prior to the imposition of the 1986 restrictions and they made it clear that they intended to introduce controls of their own in retaliation. These were announced at the very end of 1986, and 200 per cent punitive duties were proposed for a range of food and drink products including wine, gin and cheese. Because the USA is a major economic power, it can impose controls which directly hurt other aspects of the EC economy, which in turn add to the burden on EC citizens of the CAP. The American threat led to the Community moderating its proposals, and some outside suppliers were allowed into the Iberian market.

4.9 Comecon and the EC

Trade relations with the Council for Mutual Economic Assistance (CMEA) or more usually referred to as Comecon, reflect a major gap in the Community's CCP. Trade relations between the two economic groups are very limited in a direct sense, because the Comecon countries have been reluctant to acknowledge the legitimacy of the EC in political terms. Comecon does not have direct dealing with the GATT either, so that trade links tend to be bilateral with Community governments and companies dealing with state organisations. While trade with Comecon countries is significant for the EC, it represents a far more important place for the Eastern bloc, amounting to about 25 per cent of their trade. The EC takes between 40 and 60 per cent of Comecon exports of manufactured products, and energy sales are an important source of foreign exchange earnings, particularly to the Soviet Union.

After the 1950s, the Comecon counties abandoned much of their reluctance to import Western goods. The superiority of Western technology and the desire to expand their domestic production led to the following of an import growth strategy. They saw technology transfer as a means of updating the range and quality of production. To pay for this strategy, they needed to export goods to the West which were saleable. One method of payment was buy back. In return for the provision of plant and machinery, the output of that production was used for payment. Areas like chemicals are particularly suitable. In the 1970s a heavy reliance was placed upon the use of credit to finance the purchase of capital goods, but as the world economy slowed down, the ability to pay diminished. This led to a debt crisis, particularly for Poland. The more general effect was that the strategy of import-led growth became less viable. This was in part due to the unwillingness of the West to accept Comecon goods, particularly in sensitive areas like textiles, where quotas were applied. Added to this, doubts were raised about the suitability of some of the technology within Comecon. Not only was it on occasions rather dated, but there was a limit to how usefully it could be applied, given the managerial failings within the system.

Almost inevitably, East–West trade has a political dimension to it. Promoting trade by the use of credit has been used to ease political tension in the past. Most recently, however, trade sanctions have been used to express distaste of Soviet policy with regard to Afghanistan and of Polish martial law. Underlying these issues is a more general fear that trade is being used to support hostile powers. In particular the issue of high technology being made available to the Soviets has caused alarm in the USA. The fear is that many products have a twofold usability, that is, civilian products are being used for military purposes. European suppliers are less sensitive to this issue, and yet rely on US patents. Any prohibition by the USA on the export of technology gives rise to charges of technology imperialism. There is great resentment at the politicis-

ation of what many EC members see as simple commercial transactions. As long as hostility between the two superpowers remains,
it is likely that the EC will be stuck unwillingly in the middle on
the issue of trade.

4.10   Developing countries and the EC

The developing nations of the world are often characterised by low
incomes per head, inadequate infrastructure, poor health care,
malnutrition and starvation, subsistence agriculture and, in many
cases, appalling urban conditions. In the past a number of them
were colonial territories of EC member states, although the degree
of involvement varies considerably. There are a wide variety of
ways to improve the conditions within these countries, and the EC
offers help in the form of both trade and aid. Because many developing countries are not good at exporting onto the world markets
unless, of course, they are endowed with scarce mineral resources,
positive trade discrimintion is regarded as a valuable aid to
development.

The EC's trade policy with the Third World comprises over 20
commercial and financial links ordered in a complex hierarchy of
privilege. The best placed in this hierarchy are the African, Carib-
bean and Pacific (ACP) states who make up the signatories of the
Lomé Convention. These states are predominantly the former
colonies of France and the UK. It was France which was instru-
mental in wishing to keep closer ties with former colonies once they
had achieved independence. This led to the Yaoundé Conventions
of 1963 and 1969, which offered access to EC markets at a reduced
tariff, and the eventual elimination of tariffs on non-agricultural
products. Aid was also offered as part of the package. The Yaoundé
Conventions were criticised for their neo-colonialist conditions,
particularly the insistence that tariff concessions be reciprocated.
The Lomé Conventions differ from these provisions. They along
with all current EC agreements with the Third World, offer tariff
concessions on a non-reciprocal basis. The only requirement is that
Community exports into these markets are not dealt with more
harshly than those from other sources.

There have been three Lomé Conventions to date. The first ran
from 1975 to 1980 and had an aid endowment of ECU 3.45 billion,
the second ran for 1980 to 1985 and had an aid endowment of
ECU. 5.7 billion. The most recent Lomé Convention ran from
March 1985 and will finish in February 1990 with ECU 8.5 billion.

The value of the aid endowment is reduced by the fact that the membership of Lomé has increased and, of course, inflation has also reduced its real worth. Two-thirds of the 66 participants in Lomé III come from Black Africa, making it a predominantly African–EC convention. There are enormous differences in the size of the states involved, ranging from 67 million for Nigeria to the tiny populations of the Pacific islands. The degree of dependence on EC trade also varies considerably, with Togo being 90 per cent dependent while Bahamas sends only 3 per cent of exports to the EC.

Since their inception the Lomé Conventions have been criticised for not doing enough to promote trade with the Community. While ACP exports to the EC increased in value by 51 per cent (excluding petroleum products), between 1976 and 1983, their share of EC imports fell from 6.3 to 4.5 per cent. Exports from the ACP to the EC actually fell by volume in the worst of the recession in 1981. Although the Community claims that 99.5 per cent of ACP exports by value enter the EC duty free, the rest being covered by the CAP, it is clear that this is not the entire picture. First, the agricultural trade might be far higher if it was not for variable levies and quota restrictions. Second, the free access for industrial goods is restricted by requirements with regard to rules of origin. All products can contain up to 5 per cent of 'foreign' components and still be regarded as that country's products. This restricts the attractiveness of these countries to overseas investors who might wish to have assembly operations in ACP states. Under Lomé III the situation has improved because the rules of origin governing cameras, loudspeakers, telescopes and so on have been relaxed.

The Community claims that ACP failure to export to the EC markets is probably the result of inappropriate domestic policies, but access to the markets has not been generous, and in one case, that of Mauritius, a country has been asked to accept a VER on textiles. Added to this the benefit of tariff-free access has been eroded, firstly by the continuing tariff reductions negotiated under the GATT. Secondly, the value of any concessions is in any case reduced by offering tariff cuts to others. Each expansion of the Community increases the number of tariff-free exporters, even if the market has expanded. Also, EFTA countries have unrestricted access for industrial goods and many Mediterranean countries enjoy tariff-free access. Finally, although nowhere near as generous, the EC offers a Generalised System of Preferences (GSP) scheme which has a very wide geographic coverage. Under the GSP, tariff-free access is offered to EC markets for semi-manufactured and manufactured products, but is subject to a quota. Once the quota is reached, then the full tariff might be imposed. Under the GSP, sensitive areas of trade like textiles are substantially controlled, so restricting the generosity of the scheme.

4.11 Conclusion

Each new trade agreement and trade restrictions, applied either at the national or Community level, complicates the EC's trade relations. The result is that the CCP is extremely difficult to evaluate, especially as it contains within it a strong political element. The EC's contribution towards free trade is likewise difficult to judge. Quite clearly the Community is no more protectionist than many of its major trading rivals, the exception to this being in the area of agricultural products, where the EC's activities are not only disruptive, but do a great deal of damage to its other trading interests.

The temptation for the major trading blocks to take action against what appear to be unfair trading practices, adds a new urgency to the current GATT round. Despite the protestations of the Japanese that they are taking action to correct their huge trade surpluses by opening up their markets, and by allowing the value of their currency to rise, their measures are frequently seen as being a case of 'too little, too late'. The EC's CCP has a vital role to play in maintaining free trade, in that it must keep a balance between firm action against those countries which adopt protectionist policies, and ensuring that individual members do not take to using unilateral action to resolve individual trade problems. The increasing use of VERs by members undermines the CCT to the extent to which commercial policy ceases to be common at all. In this respect the action by the UK Government to try to open up the Japanese telecommunications market in 1987 is symptomatic of the problem. The way forward with a problem of this type must surely be by joint Community action, rather than relying on an individual country reponse.

4.12 References

1. R C Hine 1985 *The Political Economy of European Trade*, p 224. Wheatsheaf.

2. S A B Page 1981 The revival of protectionism and its consequence for Europe *Journal of Common Market Studies*, XX no (1) 29.
3. Ernest-Ulrich Persmann 1985 'International and European foreign trade law: GATT dispute settlement proceedings against the EEC' *Common Market Law Review*, Vol 22 p 441.
4. Ann D Morgan 1984 Protectionism and European trade in manufactures *National Institute Economic Review*, August p 45.

Chapter five
The European Monetary System – settling for less

The EMS was launched on 13 March 1979. Its broad aim was to create a zone of monetary stability within Europe. That is, it was an attempt to move towards a more stable exchange rate regime within the Community. Along with this, and a major requirement for the system's success, it was hoped that there would be greater coordination of national economic policies. Finally, there were expectations that the EMS might become part of a step-by-step approach to complete monetary integration within the EC.

When the EC was launched in 1958, the main preoccupation was the formation of the Common Market. There was no specific provision in the Treaty of Rome for the coordination of macro-economic policies; for this was considered to be largely the business of nation states. The Six, with the exception of Italy, enjoyed balance of payments surpluses, although full convertibility from one currency to another had not been achieved. Harmonisation of exchange rate policy was understandably not regarded as a priority, as this was the era of fixed exchange rates organised by the International Monetary Fund (IMF) under the Bretton Woods agreement of 1944.

Towards the end of the 1960s, the stability of the Bretton Woods system started to evaporate. In 1967 the pound sterling was devalued, and in 1969 so was the French franc, also in that year the West German mark was revalued. This instability of European currencies made it difficult to sustain the price structure of the CAP and also looked like affecting other areas of trade. Partly in response to this, the first attempt at monetary integration, the European Monetary Union (EMU), was launched in 1972. This was an ambitious scheme which aimed to achieve permanently fixed and totally convertible exchange rates by 1980. The EMU initiative was short-lived. It started to disintegrate within weeks, and finally collapsed in the wake of the floating of the US dollar and the 1973–4 oil crisis.

The EMS is therefore the second attempt at some kind of monetary integration within the EC. It contrasts with the EMU, in that in the short term at least, it is far less ambitious. It is still viewed by many as a technical operation to smooth exchange rates within the EC, rather than being part of a grand design. Settling for less, at least in the short term, may well have helped its survival through very difficult times.

In analysing the EMS, this chapter will first of all discuss the problem of floating exchange rates. It will then analyse the rationale for monetary integration. This will be followed by an assessment of its success. Finally, the chapter will look at ways in which the EMS might be developed.

5.1 The exchange rate problem

The exchange rate is simply the price of one currency in terms of another, for example £1 may be equal to $1.40, It is, however, an important price, largely because it determines the price at which goods and services are traded internationally. If the exchange-rate system is working correctly, then goods should cost roughly the same price in all countries, after allowing for transport costs and the effects of taxation. If, however, a currency is overvalued, imported goods will be cheap, and exports will be overpriced and harder to sell. As a consequence industry may well be harmed. If the currency is undervalued, imported goods will be expensive, so that the consumer will be worse off; however, exporting will be easier.

Under the system of floating exchange rates that became widespread in 1973, the value of a currency was determined by market forces. The system was supposed to have certain advantages. Among these were:

1. The conduct of domestic economic policy would not be constrained by balance of payments problems.
2. The economy would be isolated from the worst effects of trade shocks.
3. The destabilising effects of foreign monetary disturbances would be avoided.

The reality of floating exchange rates was somewhat different, with the world finance system demonstrating the same degree of interdependence as in the past. For example, the high US interest rates of the mid 1980s dominated world interest rates. The size of international capital flows is such that countries simply have to accept the exchange rate given to them by the market. The London currency market alone, handles $90 billion worth of business on an average day, compared to $50 billion for New York and $48 billion for Tokyo. This has often given rise to overshooting, that is, the overvaluation or undervaluation of a currency for a period of time. Such movements reflect the fact that short-term exchange rates are frequently determined by the demand and supply of internationally mobile money and capital, rather than by trade in goods. An illustration of this would be the performance of the British pound, which rose in value by 40 per cent in the two years to 1981, and then fell 30 per cent over the next four years. These kind of movements are almost impossible to predict and are difficult for an individual country's foreign trade sector to cope with. In particular, small and medium-sized companies may be disadvantaged in that they lack the experience or resources to cope with the fluctuations. Curiously, however, there is no conclusive evidence that floating rates are harmful in general to trade. Finally, it is clear that economies are still subject to balance of payments crises and that no economy can be isolated from trade or monetary shocks. Floating exchange rates simply have not delivered on their promise.

5.2. The rationale for monetary integration

An alternative to the system of floating exchange rates would appear to be a return to fixed exchange rates. Despite the criticism of them in the past, because of their constraining effects on economies, they are now generally regarded as an infinitely preferable system. When exchange rates were fixed, under the IMF, the volume of world trade grew by 7.5 per cent per annum, while under the system of floating rates, world trade grew only by 3.3 per cent per annum. This does not mean that floating exchange rates caused the slow-down in trade growth, but it is the case that fixed rates are associated with better times. The climate is not right for a major reform of the world monetary system, despite the deficiencies of the present system. An alternative to this is monetary integration on a European basis, building on the political and economic achievements gained to date.

Complete monetary integration is achieved when either exchange rates are permanently fixed, or just one currency exists. Along with this there must not be restrictions on the movement of capital. The activities of central banks would need to be coordinated, or perhaps, a single European central bank would need to be created. Finally, foreign exchange reserves would need to be pooled in order to defend the fixed rates or common currency. Reforms of this nature are fundamental, because they imply a major shift of economic sovereignty away from the nation state. Full monetary integration must therefore be associated with considerable progress made in other areas of integration.

Achieving monetary union would undoubtedly help to promote political unity within Europe. Apart from this general advantage, there are specific benefits which have been claimed. First of all, if a single currency was in use, one of the costs of selling in other EC markets would disappear. Even if the national currencies remained, the cost would be reduced. Secondly, the degree of certainty in trade would be greatly increased, so that companies would not find suddenly that prices had changed due to exchange-rate movements. Thirdly, the exchange rate might be more stable in relation to countries outside the EC.

Finally, it would allow capital to move to the place where it achieved the greatest return, and perhaps encourage larger capital issues to take place. This would encourage the scale of investment required to take full advantage of economies of scale.

The case against such development revolves around the issue of national sovereignty. First of all, monetary integration greatly constrains national policy makers, because it takes away their ability to decide on such issues as what might be the best rate of inflation or demand in an economy. Secondly, there is the issue of what constitutes an optimum currency area. Participation in an area using one currency gives advantages, but it takes away from policy makers the right to devalue. Balance of payments deficits may occur in some regions of the currency area, but will not be reflected in an exchange-rate depreciation. If wage rates are inflexible, and the opportunity to devalue does not exist, deflation and unemployment will follow as money leaves the region. This suggests that unless the deflation works, then the unemployment may be long term indeed. It is a problem that might be solved by the active use of regional policy. But if inter-regional transfers of funds do not compensate for the payments deficit then it is a question of offsetting the gains from trade against the costs of a totally fixed exchange rate. It may, therefore, be in the interest of some economies to stay separate from the permanent monetary arrangement.

5.3 From EMU to EMS

The EMU, when it was launched in 1972, had within it the original Six members of the EC plus the applicant states, the UK, Ireland and Denmark. Currencies were tied within a band which had a gap of no more than $2\frac{1}{4}$ per cent between the strongest and weakest. Because of its diagrammatic appearance, it quickly acquired the nickname of 'the snake', which applies to the EMS currencies today. The value of the snake was then held within a limit of no more than $2\frac{1}{4}$ per cent above or below the US dollar. This was the so-called tunnel (Fig. 5.1).

The EMU had a number of weaknesses. Despite its aim of monetary integration by 1980, there was no formal commitment to harmonise domestic economic policies in order to achieve this. Added to this was the fact that the system placed the burden of adjustment on countries with weak currencies. They were expected to keep their exchange rates up in value, rather than the burden being shared as might be expected if the policy had a serious purpose. Countries with strong currencies might offer support for weak currencies, but they were under no obligation to keep the value of their exchange rate down. Belatedly, but of only minor significance, the European Monetary Cooperation Fund (EMCF) was set up in April 1973. This was concerned with the management of monetary support for the EMU, and was to continue in existence in the EMS.

The major factor which caused the decline of the EMU was the collapse of confidence in the US dollar. Not only was the dollar an integral part of the EMU, but it was also at the centre of the fixed exchange rate system. The stability of the dollar was therefore essential for success. In the period that followed, exchange rates became particularly unstable, especially after the oil crisis of

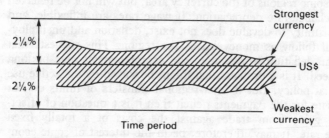

Fig. 5.1 The snake and the tunnel

1973–74. Many economies faced severe balance of payments difficulties, and inflation became a world-wide problem. All that survived of the EMU was a snake which contained the Benelux currencies and the Danish krone attached to the dominant West German mark.

Launching the EMS

Despite an unpromising experience with its first attempt at monetary integration, Roy Jenkins, the President of the Commission, suggested the revival of the EMU as early as October 1977. Jenkins was searching for the kind of initiative which might get the process of political integration going again. The collaboration of President Giscard d'Estaing and Chancellor Schmidt which put forward the EMS idea in 1978, envisaged a much more limited initiative. Their aim was to create a zone of monetary stability which would benefit Community trade.

At that time it was clear that conditions were better for such a project. First of all, many countries were disillusioned by the effects of floating exchange rates. Not only did they appear to impede trade, but West Germany felt a need to protect the mark against being forced upward in value by the weakening dollar. Secondly, there were signs that the economies of Europe were starting to converge. In particular, most governments saw curing inflation as their major priority.

Enthusiasm for the EMS was not universal. Ireland had to be bribed to participate, Italy was able to enter on differing terms to other members. The UK joined, but decided not to participate in the Exchange Rate Mechanism (ERM). This was probably a politically motivated decision. The right terms were probably available, but the Callaghan Government feared that full membership might divide the Labour Party prior to the general election. Also, there was the fear that if the pound was overvalued it might inhibit dealing with rising unemployment. Once the decision to stay out had been made, the strength of sterling as a petro currency, and the wish of the Conservative Government (in power after May 1979) to use monetary policy to control inflation, made full membership unlikely in the short term. The value of the pound was pushed up, firstly by the large balance of payments surplus generated by North Sea oil and, secondly by the high interest rates used to control monetary growth. The high value of sterling did permit cheap imports into the UK and was consequently welcomed by the Thatcher Government as it helped to moderate inflation. A high price was paid, however, for it undoubtedly contributed to the severity of UK unemployment. It has been suggested that membership of the ERM might have helped too by capping the value of the currency, but if the pound had been a member, it may have created the kind of stress that would have resulted in the ERM being pulled apart.

The structure of the EMS

The EMS contains three specific operational features. They are:

1. The ECU, a composite of EMS currencies.
2. The ERM, a system of fixing participating currencies within a narrow $2\frac{1}{4}$ per cent band.
3. The EMCF.

Membership of the EMS is not obligatory for members of the EC, and it is possible to be a member of all or part of it. When the EMS was launched, the UK decided not to participate in the ERM, and the Greek drachma did not join the ECU until its first five-year review in September 1984 (there was an initial six-month review). The Spanish peseta and Portuguese escudo may become part of the EMS when it is considered that their currencies have sufficient stability to survive within the system. The Spanish, in particular, indicated an enthusiasm to become full members of the EMS, but perhaps with a wider margin within the ERM similar to the 6 per cent being operated for Italy.

The ECU

When the EC was first launched, the first unit of account (UA) was fixed at the same value as the US dollar. This relationship collapsed in the 1970s when several UAs came into existence as a result of the system of floating exchange rates. The confusion ended in 1979 when the ECU was introduced. It is made up of a trade-weighted basket of currencies whose composition is as given in Table 5.1.

A request for an early review of the above weights may be made if the importance of the currency changes significantly.

The ECU has been assigned four functions within the EMS. They are to act as:

1. The denominator for the exchange-rate mechanism.
2. The basis of the divergence indicator.
3. The denominator for operations in both the intervention and credit mechanisms.

Table 5.1 Composition of the ECU Nov. 1986

Countries	Weights
German mark	34.06
French franc	19.06
British pound	12.93
Dutch florin	10.76
Italian lira	8.93
Belgian franc	9.48
Danish krone	2.8
Greek drachma	0.84
Irish pound	1.14
Luxembourg franc	—

4. A means of settlement between monetary authorities in the Community.

Apart from its official functions, the ECU has been developed for private purposes, and these will be discussed later.

The Exchange Rate Mechanism

The ERM is a system of fixing members' exchange rates within a narrow band, so that the divergence between the strongest and weakest is not more than 2.25 per cent. The exception to this rule being Italy, which is allowed a 6 per cent divergence.

Intervention to maintain the system is compulsory when the divergence between the strongest and weakest looks like being greater than the permitted limit. The central bank with the strong currency must buy the currency of the weak; and in turn the central bank with the weak currency sells the strong currency using borrowed funds as required.

The use of the ECU makes the system different from the EMU snake, for it is a device to measure the position of a currency relative to the Community average. The actual amount that a currency can deviate from the ECU is less than 2.25 per cent because the currency is part of the ECU. Thus a small currency like the Irish pound can diverge by 2.22 per cent. A heavily weighted currency like the West German mark can, however, only diverge from the ECU by 1.53 per cent, and at the same time keep within the 2.25 per cent limit with other currencies.

A novel feature of the system is the use of the ECU-based divergence indicator. When a currency reaches 75 per cent of its maximum spread within the mechanism – the so-called divergence threshold – there is a presumption that action will be taken to correct this situation. But corrective action is not compulsory until the actual maximum spread is reached. This is complicated by the fact that the pound and the lira have not stayed within the 2.25 per cent limit. Their fluctuations beyond the 2.25 per cent are ignored when calculating the divergence indicator. Sensible though this correction is, it can result in currencies remaining beyond the 75 per cent divergence threshold, as was the Belgian franc for a period of time, in the first five years of the life of the EMS. Fig. 5.2 shows the system for two currencies.

One of the reasons for the ERM being in this form was that the adjustment process would be more equally shared between strong and weak currencies. In reality, the system has not given the signals that were desired, and the burden of adjustment still falls on the weak currencies. This in turn has led to a strengthening of the position of the German monetary authorities. Because of the low rates of inflation and good balance of payments record in West Germany, the Bundesbank tends to lead the EMS's exchange-rate policy relative to currencies like the US dollar.

The EMCF

The EMCF existed in a more limited form under the EMU. Under

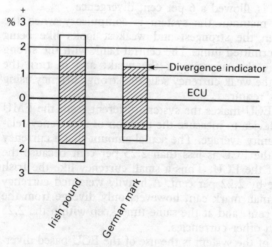

Fig. 5.2 The ERM

the EMS, it receives 20 per cent of the value of each member's gold and foreign currency reserves, and they receive ECUs in return. The deposits are not permanent, but are swopped on a revolving basis every three months. The hope was that the EMCF would become a European Monetary Fund (EMF) within two years, in which case the swop would become permanent. In 1980, however, the EMF proposal was postponed until a more appropriate time, and this time seems to be regarded as being increasingly long term. The Single European Act makes the prospects for an EMF even more remote, as it now requires an amendment to the Treaties.

The EMCF does not act independently, but is responsible for administering three types of credit mechanism. They are:

1. *Very short-term financing*. This is automatically available for financing obligatory intervention to maintain the value of a currency. Debts have to be repaid, usually within a time period of between one and a half to two and a half months. The usefulness of this facility is limited, because in most cases monetary authorities prefer to intervene before this point. If they do not, they risk speculative pressures building up against the currency.

2. *Short-term monetary support*. This allows central banks to borrow in order to finance temporary balance of payments difficulties. Loans are initially for three months, but may be renewed once. It is a facility that has been used only very infrequently.

3. *Medium-term financial assistance*. These are loans with conditions attached; made in ECUs. Finance is granted for between two and five years. Once again, it has only rarely been used.

In addition to the above, there exists the *Community loan mechanism*. The Community is able to borrow on world markets up to ECU 6 billion, which can be re-lent to member states on the same terms. Conditions are normally attached to these medium-term loans, although the severity of them may differ. In 1983 the French borrowed ECU 4 billion with only a vague commitment to austerity. The ECU 1.75 billion loan granted to the Greek Government in 1985 in contrast, contained far more detailed conditions.

Assessing the success of the EMS

When the EMS was launched the worst effects of the 1973–74 oil crisis were over, but in 1979 there was yet another sharp rise in the price of oil. The second oil shock led to a sharp deterioration in the terms of trade in most European countries, and helped to speed up inflation rates. From 1980 onward the US dollar rose in value consistently over a five-year period. Although this resulted in deterioration in the US balance of payments, it helped to provide useful markets for EC products, and at the same time stopped speculation pushing the value of the West German mark upward within the EMS. Therefore, there were factors which both helped and hindered the progress of the EMS.

The most important objective in the short term was to provide a zone of monetary stability, although this was not likely to be achieved without some degree of policy coordination. As Table 5.2 shows, there were eleven changes in central rates in eight years.

Table 5.2   % changes in central rates of the EMS

Date	Revalued (%)		Devalued (%)	
24.09.79	German mark	+2	Danish krone	−3
30.11.79			Danish krone	−5
23.03.81			Italian lira	−6
05.10.81	German mark	+5.5	French france	−3
	Dutch guilder	+5.5	Italian lira	−3
22.02.82			Belgian franc	−8.5
			Lux. franc	−8.5
			Danish krone	−3
12.06.82	German mark	+4.25	French franc	−5.75
	Dutch guilder	+4.25	Italian lira	−2.75
21.03.83	German mark	+5.5	French franc	−2.5
	Dutch guilder	+3.5	Irish pound	−3.5
	Belgian franc	+1.5	Italian lira	−2.5
	Lux. franc	+1.5		
	Danish krone	+2.5		
21.07.85	All currencies except lira	+2	Italian lira	−6
07.04.86	German mark	+3	French franc	−3
	Dutch guilder	+3		
	Danish krone	+1		
	Belgian franc	+1		
	Lux. franc	+1		
04.08.86			Irish pound	−8
12.01.87	German mark	+3		
	Dutch guilder	+3		
	Belgian franc	+2		
	Lux. franc	+2		

Superficially, it looks as though the system was particularly unstable. However, it is possible to identify three distinct periods within that eight years. They are:

1. *1979 to March 1981* – only minor changes in central rates.
2. *March 1981 to March 1983* – significant changes due to the French Pursuing an expansive economic policy.
3. *March 1983 to 1987* – only four realignments with nominal rates showing great stability.

In this third period, the stability of nominal exchange rates was seen as an indication of the success of the system. The slowing down of inflation rates within the EC is regarded as evidence of policy convergence within the EMS. However, monetary discipline is also evident elsewhere, as slowing down of inflation rates is observable in many economies. Despite the downward trend in inflation, there are significant differences in the performance of EMS economies, so that although nominal exchange rates are stable, real exchange rates (i.e. nominal rates adjusted for inflation) were not. It would appear that real exchange rates within the EMS were not significantly more stable in the 1983–87 period than a number of other currencies – the notable exception being the US dollar.

It is the real exchange rate which is important in the medium term, because it affects the competitiveness of an economy, which in turn influences trade flows. Fig. 5.3 shows the divergence between the nominal and real exchange rates against the West German mark, between 1979 and the April 1986 realignment of the EMS. What it illustrates is that only the Dutch guilder retained its competitive edge, so that further realignments would be required to restore the competitive positions of these economies.

5.4 The developing ECU

The developing use of the ECU by European institutions and central banks was to a degree predictable. In parallel with this, however, has been the evolution of a private ECU. Private ECUs are created by the private banking system and companies and are used for both fund raising and invoicing. Their advantage is that they can be used to reduce exchange rate risk and are a useful way of avoiding exchange controls. In recent years the growth of the private ECU has been dramatic and, by 1985, assets denominated in them probably exceeded ECU 30 billion. Although there is no

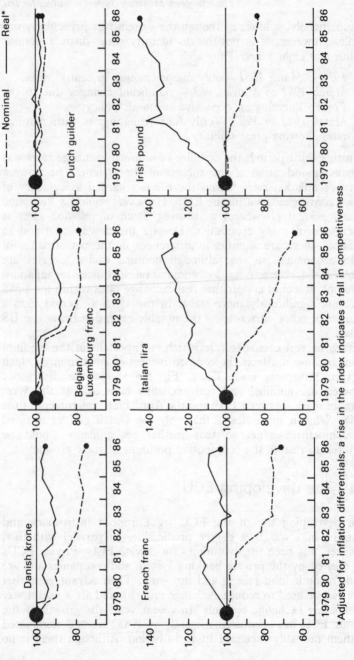

*Adjusted for inflation differentials, a rise in the index indicates a fall in competitiveness

Fig. 5.3 EMS exchange rate against the German mark (March 1979–100) Source: *The Economist,* 12 April 1986

connection between official and private ECUs, there is the hope that the two might merge to become the basis of a European currency.

The ECU is not seen by everyone as a success story. A survey of the European public's knowledge of the ECU, conducted in 1985, found that only about one-third of those questioned had even heard of it, and probably fewer knew what it was. Cynics also pointed out that the growth of the use of ECUs is an indication of a lack of progress towards monetary integration rather that a step towards a European currency. They argue that the ECU is made up of some currencies of doubtful quality, and that if progress had been made towards integration there would be no need to opt for an artificial currency.

5.5 Making the EMS work

The success of the EMS to date must be attributed to the flexibility of the approach towards monetary integration. Settling for less than the EMU has yielded more certain results. There is, however, a natural tendency to overstate these achievements, and a wish to move policy developments too quickly. A great deal of the stability and convergence that has taken place in recent years might well have been realised without the EMS. The success of the EMS lies in it not being too rigid to exploit those improved conditions. For the system to develop further, there are four major prerequisites, all of which require greater cooperation between members. These are:

1. Full participation of all EC currencies in the EMS. The persistence of the UK in particular, in remaining outside the ERM has been regarded as a vote of no confidence, and a source of discouragement to others.
2. The convergence of member economies' growth rates and inflation rates. This does not imply an automatic acceptance of the view of those countries who regard price stability as the dominant priority. The growth rates of the EMS countries has been inferior to the non-EMS industrial countries for a number of years. The loss of economic sovereignty which monetary integration implies is only likely to be fully acceptable in an era of more sustained growth.
3. A more stable relation with other West European currencies and the US dollar. This relationship with other European

currencies is important because it helps to spread the zone of stability. The problem with the dollar is that its movements can serve artificially to strengthen or weaken currencies like the German mark.

If the dollar is weak, speculators often move into marks, and as a consequence the value of the mark is forced up. This in turn causes pressure on the system.

4. Some institutional reform. Perhaps the most urgent being a more meaningful system of support for currencies facing difficulties. The proposed EMF presents a number of difficulties with regard to national sovereignty; however, a reformed EMCF might be obtainable.

5.6 Conclusion

The inclusion of the EMS in the Single European Act, undoubtedly raises the status of the mechanism. It is still the case, however, that the national monetary authorities are dominant within the system. Agreements like the Plaza Agreement arrived at in September 1985, between the major world financial powers, did not involve direct EC participation. This was a particularly important agreement, given that its purpose was to adopt a common strategy on the value of the US dollar. The most powerful central banks in Europe still see international negotiation and domestic monetary policy as an issue of national concern.

Chapter six

Regional policy: a problem of distributional politics

by Jill Preston

From its inception the EC has shown a clear commitment to the reduction of regional imbalances. The preamble to the Treaty of Rome states that the members: '. . . are anxious to strengthen the unity of their economies and to ensure their harmonious development by reducing the differences between the various regions and by mitigating the backwardness of the less favoured regions'.

But the Treaty makes no provision for a Community policy in the regional sphere. In fact, running through the Treaty of Rome is a fundamental contradiction. On the one hand, there is the commitment to free trade, free competition and free factor mobility, whereas on the other hand, regional policies represent a threat to the principle of free competition and trade. This commitment to regional policy emerges as a series of exceptions to the various rules of the Community. For example, Articles 80, 92 and 226 allow member states to use regional aids that are otherwise incompatible with the Treaty.

Regional development is a politically sensitive policy area, and in the main, member governments have been unwilling to relinquish power to Community institutions, particularly during a period of economic recession. An examination of EC regional policy has to be viewed from within the general context of Community policy making, involving as it does conflicting interests and bargaining between the member states and between the members and various EC institutions.

By definition, the Community's regional policy is concerned with removing the major disparities between the regions. But the unsystematic development of this policy and its limited and vague policy objectives makes evaluation difficult. Fig. 6.1 shows the diversity of living standards within the regions of the Community in 1983. The Commission has attempted to pursue a number of objectives, for example the implementation of an efficient and effective policy through the coordination of various measures. But such objectives have not as yet gone beyond general statements.

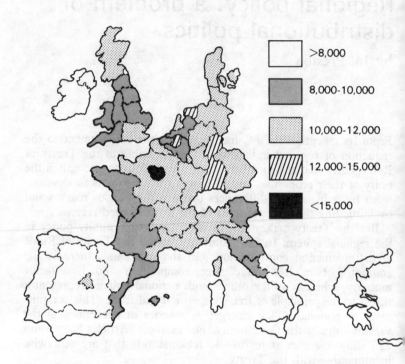

Fig. 6.1 GDP per head in the regions of the Community in 1983
Source: European File 12 1986

Key:
- >8,000
- 8,000-10,000
- 10,000-12,000
- 12,000-15,000
- <15,000

6.1 The rationale for a Community regional policy

There are a number of reasons why the Community is pursuing a regional policy. Firstly, it is argued that gross inequality between regions in any economy prevents the sound development of that economy as a whole. Secondly, it is felt that major regional differences within individual member states are harmful for the Community as a whole; countries with severe regional problems find it more difficult to control factors such as balance of payments and price stability, which are necessary requirements for a move towards economic and monetary integration. Thirdly, the Community has some responsibilities towards its poorer regions, because certain EC policies, for example the CAP, have accentuated regional inequality. Social and political factors are also relevant; for there is a feeling within the Community that serious prosperity gaps are socially unjust and politically unacceptable. The Commission wishes to develop more direct lines of communications with sub-national units of government, at both regional and local levels, and regional policy is a useful vehicle for this type of integration.

6.2 The development of regional policy

In 1970 when the regional debate gained momentum the main regional problem was the very wide disparities in the level of economic development between the various areas. The per capita GDP was six times higher in the richest Community regions of Hamburg and Paris, than in the poorer areas such as Calabria in southern Italy.

In the 1970s there were two types of problem region within the Community: the agricultural and the industrial. In the former, between 20 and 40 per cent of the working population was employed on the land, but productivity was low and most farms provided neither an adequate income nor a full-time occupation. This type of problem region was found on the periphery of the Community, for example, the Mezzogiorno in southern Italy. And with enlargement in 1973, 1983 and 1985 further poor peripheral agricultural regions were added.

The second type of problem regions were those suffering severe industrial decline which affected steel, coal, shipbuilding and textile areas in particular. By 1970 these areas were paying the price for their failure to modernise or diversify into more promising sectors. This syndrome afflicted the once prosperous coal- and steel-producing areas of Belgium and France. It was this second type of problem region found in the declining industrial areas in the north and west of England, Scotland, Wales and Northern Ireland, which became particularly significant after the first enlargement of 1973.

In the 1960s and 1970s the main objective of regional policy at the national level may be simply stated as aiming to reduce regional disparities. At the Community level there were two possible alternative lines of action. Regional policy could be limited to supplementing national measures, or a Community regional policy could have a more ambitious target of determining an EC approach within which national regional policies would be subsumed.

One of the problems that has faced the development of EC regional policy is not only the variety of regions and the lack of a clear definition of regional problems, but also the immense differences in attitude towards this policy sector in each of the member states. For in each member state there is a variety of regional aids, for example, employment subsidies and cheap loans as well as the provision of infrastructure.

It is useful to divide the development of EC regional policy into four periods viz.: 1952–70; 1971–March 1975; March 1975–1980 and 1981–86.

1952–1970

The founding fathers of the Community assumed that the process of integration plus general economic expansion would automatically close the gap between the richer and poorer regions. In the 1950s of the original Six members only Italy had a really severe regional problem. The founders felt that this one problem area could be tackled without the need for a Community regional policy, but instead it could be eased by such means as loans from the European Investment Bank (EIB) and aid from the Social Fund and other *ad hoc* measures.

The Community's regional policy advanced little during the 1960s. This was due in part to the relative prosperity of the decade. But in 1967 a new Directorate-General of the EC was created within the Commission (DG XVI) which was responsible for regional affairs. By the end of this decade it was clear that the high rate of economic growth had not led to the convergence of regional economic welfare. In October 1969 the Commission sent a memorandum to the Council of Ministers arguing that regional disparities held back the successful implementation of other common policies.

1971–March 1975

In the early 1970s progress achieved in this policy sector was due to three main factors. Firstly, in 1971 the Council committed itself to creating an EMU by 1980, and regional imbalances could be a major obstacle. Secondly, by this time enlargement negotiations had started and two of the three newcomers, Ireland and the UK, had considerable regional problems. And finally in 1971 the Competition Directorate proposed that the Community should control the level and type of national regional aids.

During 1972 regional policy became the focus of increasing attention, and from 1971 a regional focus was incorporated into the reformed ESF. By the early 1970s there was a range of policies and financial instruments which had a regional dimension, but what was lacking was an overall coordinated regional strategy.

In May 1973, DG XVI produced an important report 'On the regional problems of the enlarged Community'. This document sets out the moral, environmental and economic reasons for having an EC regional policy; it also recommends guidelines for the operation of a European regional development fund and methods for coordinating national regional policies.

But by the autumn of 1973 it was clear that there were crucial problems to be overcome in the development of regional policy. There were substantial differences of opinion among the Nine members concerning both the principles as well as the detailed proposals. Areas of disagreement focused on the size of the ERDF the definition of areas eligible for assistance and the method of allocating aid between member states. There were a number of factors which made progress to a solution that much more difficult. The Yom Kippur War and the ensuing oil embargo of the Arab oil producers became a major concern. The abandonment in the short term of the commitment to establish a monetary union also helped to slow down the pace of negotiations. In addition, in March 1972, a minority Labour Government took office and pledged to renegotiate the UK's terms of membership. With the withdrawal of pressure by the UK, the impetus to solve the issue was lost for the time being.

During 1972, George Thomson, the Regional Affairs Commissioner, with the support of the Irish and Italian Governments kept the issues of regional policy on the political agenda. At the end of 1974 the Irish and Italians agreed to attend the Paris Summit only if the other member governments would give an immediate commitment to set up the regional fund. The Summit agreed to the creation of the ERDF for an experimental period of three years. After conciliation between the Council and the European Parliament the ERDF was formally established in March 1975.

March 1975–1980

By March 1975 the Community's regional policy had three main strands:

1. The ERDF;
2. Coordination of the regional policies of individual member states;
3. Coordination of Community policies with regional effects.

By the creation of the ERDF, the Community had for the first time adopted a specific measure designed to alleviate its regional problems. But of crucial significance the purpose of the ERDF was to support national regional policies, and no attempt was made to identify a Community approach within which national policies would have been subsumed. The ERDF is the main financial instrument of EC regional policy; for this reason this chapter will concentrate on the development of the ERDF.

The ERDF was small, being 4.8 per cent of the Community budget in 1975. After the three-year experimental period it obtained permanent status. Until 1979 the entire ERDF operated under a system of national quotas where each member was entitled to claim up to a specific amount of the total. For example, in 1976 the UK could claim 28 per cent of the ERDF, whereas Italy and West Germany could claim up to 40 per cent and 6.4 per cent respectively. The system of national quotas had a number of implications; for example, the potential for DG XVI to play an active role in project choice was much reduced if members submitted claims that amounted exactly to their quotas. The map of eligible regions that had been drawn up was fairly open ended; in the UK this meant the assisted areas.

The ERDF had three categories:

(a) Industrial, handicraft or service activities which are economically sound and which benefit from state regional aid. Projects must either create or avoid the loss of at least ten jobs.
(b) Investment in infrastructure linked with the development of a given area or region and totally or partially financed by public authorities or by any other agency responsible for the building of infrastructure.
(c) Investment in rural infrastructure in hill and mountain areas and certain less favoured areas.

In theory no more than 70 per cent of the ERDF should go on infrastructure projects, but in practice over 80 per cent has been used for this purpose. The remaining sections of this chapter will concentrate on this part of the ERDF.

Until 1984 the ERDF could contribute 30 per cent of the expenditure incurred by public authorities for infrastructure investments of less than ECU 10 million and between 10 and 30 per cent for investments over ECU 10 million. The original intention was that money from the ERDF would be added to that given by member states under their own regional aid schemes. But the ERDF does not impose vertical additionality, for in the case of industrial, handicraft and service projects it gives member states the option of paying the ERDF contribution to the investors or keeping it as partial reimbursement of its own incentives. No member state has chosen the first alternative. In the case of infrastructure a public authority that receives ERDF aid for a capital project is allowed to use the grant to reduce interest charges and debt services. So in the UK as in the other member states the concept of additionality is an illusion, the greater benefit accrues to the Treasury rather than to the public authority. The ability of the Community institutions to establish and enforce priorities for ERDF assistance is severely restricted by the extent that individual member states bypass the 'additional' character of the ERDF.

In 1977 the Commission put forward proposals for reforming the ERDF. After two years of very difficult negotiations most of these proposals were adopted. The Commission suggested that a report on the social and economic trends in the regions should be published, from this document priorities and guidelines could be proposed by the Council. The first Periodic Report was published in 1980 and the second Report was published in 1984.

A major proposal put forward by the Commission at this time was the idea of a non-quota element of the ERDF. This element was intended to finance, with national authorities, projects whose aim was to deal with specific Community regional development measures. These measures were intended to overcome problems associated with Community decisions in areas such as changing economic trading patterns. In negotiations there was much opposition to this non-quota section, as some members felt that this could be the beginning of a Community regional policy. The compromise reached was that the non-quota section was limited to 5 per cent of the ERDF budget. Each non-quota project required the unanimous approval of the Council of Ministers; measures approved have included projects to assist areas seriously affected by the restructuring of the steel industry, as well as areas hard hit by a declining shipbuilding industry.

The revised regulations of 1979 changed the definition of eligibility from purely economic infrastructure such as roads, ports and industrial sites to that which contributes to the development of the region in which it is situated. This alteration opened the possibility of financing such investments as environmental improvements and tourist infrastructure. The 1979 amendments were little more than marginal adjustments to existing regulations rather than a major step forward in the development of an effective Community regional policy.

1981–1986

By the beginning of the 1980s there was growing disenchantment with the operation of regional policy in general and with the ERDF in particular. Critics argued that the ERDF was too small; it was 7.5 per cent of the total budget in 1985, and that it was too thinly spread. It covered some 60 per cent of the geographical area and approximately 40 per cent of the population of the Community. It was also argued that the system of national quotas inadequately related to the nature and seriousness of regional disparities. In addition, there was criticism from some quarters that the national governments had too tight a control over this policy.

During this period the reform of the ERDF went through two stages: the Commission's original proposals for reform were published in October 1981, and an amended version was published in November 1983. The new regulations appeared in the *Official Journal* in June 1984, and came into effect on 1 January 1985.

The 1981 proposal was both radical and controversial. For example, it was suggested that regional policy should concentrate on job creation and a drastic reduction of eligible regions was proposed. The Commission also recommended fundamental changes to the non-quota section of the ERDF. It was suggested that this section should have its resources increased from 5 per cent to 20 per cent of the total Fund.

It is not surprising in view of the radical nature of these suggestions and their far-reaching implications for the power relationships existing between the Commission and the member states, that the Council of Ministers did not give its authority to the proposal. Two of the main problems were, firstly, certain members such as West Germany and the Netherlands would have been excluded from the quota section. And secondly, the proposal to increase the non-quota section from 5 per cent to 20 per cent would have meant that the Commission would have controlled a major proportion of

Fund allocations. In addition, at this time the EC budget and the CAP were once again becoming major issues requiring the attention of the Council of Ministers.

In November 1983, the Commission suggested an amended version of the 1981 proposal. A major feature of the 1983 proposal was the recommendation that the distinction between the quota and non-quota sections of the ERDF should be abolished. It was suggested that Fund aid should be concentrated on the least advantaged regions but that no member state should be completely excluded. The Commission proposed that the ERDF should be distributed on the basis of a system of flexible quotas. Table 6.1 shows the ranges of these quotas for each of the member states.

Table 6.1 The quota ranges suggested in the 1983 proposal

Member state	Lower limit (%)	Upper limit (%)
Belgium	0.85	1.20
Denmark	0.81	1.14
West Germany	3.55	4.81
Greece	11.05	15.60
France	10.44	14.74
Ireland	5.05	7.13
Italy	30.17	42.59
Luxembourg	0.06	0.08
Netherlands	0.95	1.34
UK	20.23	28.56

Source: Commission of the EC *COM (83) 649 Final* November 1983

To replace the quota and non-quota sections, the Commission proposed two types of programme: the Community programme and the national programme of Community interest. Programme financing as opposed to its support for individual projects would take up an increasing proportion of the ERDF's resources.

It was proposed that Community programmes would normally involve more than one member state and would be undertaken on the initiative of the Commission. These programmes would consist of a coordinated series of multi-annual measures directly serving EC objectives. The framework for a programme would require adoption by the Council of Ministers.

It was suggested that national programmes of Community interest would consist of systematic groups of multi-annual measures serving both national and Community objectives. Such a programme would involve part of a region or one or more regions and would include, jointly or separately: infrastructure investments, schemes for industry and services and operations to exploit the potential for internally generated development. Programmes would be undertaken on the initiative of member states, who would prepare them in association with the organisations concerned and would then present them to the Commission for assessment. These national programmes would be limited to those assisted areas designated by member states for the purpose of their regional aid schemes. By this time any national changes in the assisted areas map had to obtain the approval of the Commission. The ERDFs contribution would be 40 per cent of the total public authority expenditure if the project cost less than ECU 10 million and between 20 and 40 per cent in the case of projects costing ECU 10 million or more.

The 1983 proposal was an attempt to suggest a workable compromise which would enable a quick decision to be reached among the member states. In this general objective it was successful, for in May 1984 after negotiations within the Council of Ministers and some discussion with the European Parliament, broad agreement was reached. There were limited amendments to the proposal, but a new regulation was agreed on 18 and 19 June of that year.

The new regulation is the result of an attempt to focus aid onto the poorer regions of the Community, and by the institution of flexible quotas it is likely that DG XVI will have a greater say in project choice. But the DG has been slow to translate these changes into administrative procedures; therefore, it will be a number of years before these changes can be evaluated realistically. There are a few areas where there is still some confusion. For example, it is not clear how a member state can obtain its maximum as opposed to its minimum quota of aid.

At the end of 1984 local authorities in England were not only faced with problems associated with this new regulation, but in addition, in November 1984, the national government altered its regional assistance map, thereby making a number of local authorities ineligible for ERDF aid. Here DG XVI was slow to determine its transitional arrangements for those authorities that had lost regional assistance status.

6.3 Conclusion

Regional development is a politically sensitive policy area and the majority of member states have been unwilling to relinquish power to the EC. The Community aims to remove major disparities between the regions; one reason being that certain EC policies have accentuated these differences. In addition, the Community has attempted to coordinate the use of its various financial instruments such as the ERDF and the ESF, but this approach has posed many difficulties because of the variety of administrative and political structures within the member states.

The development of regional policy illustrates a number of the problems involved in developing common policies within the Community, for example, at every stage of its development the member states have kept a firm grip on all important aspects of the policy. To date most member states are concerned that Community policy should involve supplementing national measures, rather than pursuing the more ambitious target of determining an EC approach within which national regional policies would be subsumed. The reforms of the ERDF which were implemented in 1985 are likely to give the Commission a greater say in project choice, but these changes are only procedural and they do not take into account the regional problems resulting from the membership of Spain and Portugal.

The regional policy of the EC involves problems of distributional politics, because the main financial instrument, the ERDF is a small element of the overall budget. Thus Community regional policy can have only a marginal effect on regional development. According to the second Periodic Report, regional disparities have continued to increase over the last 10 years. Until a radical reform of the CAP has been achieved there is little prospect for increasing other funds such as the ERDF.

Chapter seven
Industrial policy

Industrial policy is designed to solve the problems of structural change facing industry. That is, it is intended to affect the supply side of the economy. Included in the list of specific industrial policy instruments are: regional aids, tax concessions, non-tariff barriers, subsidies, government controls, monopoly and restrictive practice legislation, credit policies and industrial relations legislation. Some policies are designed to improve the environment in which industry operates, and have a less specific effect. At a Community-wide level we have seen how measures to promote the internal market are designed to do this. In this chapter we will discuss the EC's competition policy which is designed to promote a free-market environment within the Community. Other policies are designed to have an impact on a particular sector of the European economy in an attempt to either speed up the pace of change in order to maintain competitiveness, or to slow down change in order to preserve jobs.

While there are very few actions of the state with regard to the economy that do not have some impact on industry, industrial policy is rarely constructed in a coherent way. Some countries such as France and Italy have traditionally taken a more interventions stance with regard to their industry. Others like West Germany have tended to rely more on a market-based strategy. Since the slow-down of the world economy in 1973, all members of the EC have operated an increasing array of policies. Some of these simply counteract the policies being operated in other states. On occasions this has led to an almost indecent auction to attract the limited amount of footloose international investment available. An example of this was the competition between member states to persuade the Japanese car producer Nissan to establish itself within their country. The result was that the company was able to maximise the available subsidy, despite the fact that it was destined to open a European plant anyway.

7.1 The rationale for an industrial policy

The origins of the EC's involvement with industrial policy can be traced back to the ECSC launched in 1951, which put the coal, iron and steel industries of its Six members under one High Authority. Although based upon one industry, the ECSC was primarily political in its purpose. Under the Treaty of Rome which brought the EEC into existence, the main emphasis was upon competition policy, without specific mention being made of industrial policy. There were, of course, important sectoral policies in the case of agriculture and transport, and great hopes were held for Euratom, which was designed to promote research and development in the peaceful use of nuclear power.

The emphasis on competition policy was understandable in the early stages of the EC's development. Generally speaking, industry was growing rapidly, and the main concern was for the operation of a competitive market as a vehicle to promote economic and political integration. It was only in the 1970s that the industries of the member states started to face a general crisis. The economic growth in the developed world slowed down, initially due to the oil crisis of 1973–74. This slow growth continued, and was accompanied by high levels of unemployment especially in the 1980s. In response to this crisis, a whole array of measures were adopted by members, and it was clear that some kind of Community response was called for. Industrial policies adopted by member states tended to renationalise problems of the European economy, and so reduce the benefits from integration. That is, member states have usurped the role of the EC in adopting purely national solutions to the problems facing their industries. A Community-wide industrial policy should:

1. Eliminate many of the conflicting rival national policies.
2. Reduce the unfairness of national policies, where the stronger states gained at the expense of weaker states.
3. Create a European-wide strategy for industry.

What a Community industrial policy cannot do, in the short term at least, is to eliminate national intervention totally. The recognition that industrial performance is not satisfactory makes state aids inevitable. Added to this the Community simply does not have the funds to launch initiatives in all sectors. It has therefore concentrated on first, competition policy, second, sectoral policies and third, promoting joint research and development projects.

7.2 Competition policy

The free-market bias of the Community is most obviously reflected in its competition policy. Article 3(f) of the Treaty of Rome calls for a system that ensures that competition in the market is not distorted. The actual rules of competition are set out in Articles 85–94 of the Treaty. These rules are directed against the activities of both companies and states, although as we shall see later the degree of success of action against states has been limited.

Controlling the activities of companies

Article 85 of the Treaty is concerned with agreements made between firms in the EC to restrict competition, while Article 86 deals with firms in a dominant position in the market. Regulation 17 of 1962 gave the Commission considerable powers to investigate and enforce the provisions of these articles. The Commission, in its investigations, is entitled to examine the books and records of companies, ask for on-the-spot explanations and enter premises. Where the law has been contravened the Commission is entitled to impose fines up to ECU 1 million, or in excess of this, providing that it does not amount to more than 10 per cent of the previous year's turnover. Appeals against the Commission's powers can be made to the ECJ. Some kind of appeal mechanism is thought to be essential, given the status of the Commission as both judge and investigator of offences.

The Commission learns about cases from information given by firms, complaints from third parties or by acting on its own initiative. It prefers not to act directly on its own initiative, because this is administratively more difficult. Inevitably there are conflicts between the legislation of member states and that of the the EC, given that most member states have some kind of legislation in this area of policy. While members can deal with cases concerning Articles 85 and 86, they are expected to bow to the superiority of the Community if the Commission decides to take a case up. Clearly the Commission faces difficulties because it is dealing with the activities of companies across 12 national boundaries. The amount of research it can do is limited, and so it tends to find itself restricted in the ground it can cover. A great deal of publicity tends to accompany the cases which the Commission regards as important, in order to maximise the demonstration effect.

Restrictive practices and Article 85

This article concerns itself with collusive agreements between two or more firms which act in such a way as to distort market competition. These agreements can be in the form of price fixing, in which case the quantity of the product sold will depend upon the demand for it at the fixed price. If market forces were in operation then the price might be lower, and the quantity sold greater. Prices can also vary according to the market in which it is being sold, so that prices might be higher in some countries than in others. Alternatively, companies might agree to restrict output or supplies to particular markets, in the hope that prices will rise. Agreements can also be made which force customers to accept conditions of sale which they might not wish to, given a free choice.

Although there is no compulsion to do so, companies are requested to notify the Commission of any agreements which might infringe Article 85. Large numbers of firms have done so in order to be considered for exemption from its effects. If the Commission is not informed of an agreement, then exemptions are not granted. Agreements which do not limit competition, and improve production and distribution of a good are generally exempt from actions under Article 85.

To illustrate the importance of the Commission's role under Article 85, it is useful to look at two cases in which prosecution was completed in 1986. The first concerns the chemical industry, which has a history of forming international cartels. In 1977, the four largest producers of polypropylene, including Shell and ICI, controlled 64 per cent of that market. In that year they made their first moves towards fixing prices. As capacity grew in the industry, more companies became involved, so that when the cartel was broken up in 1983, 15 companies were prosecuted. They had managed to double prices over a six-year period, and it was estimated that prices were regularly 25–30 per cent above what they should have been. The companies operated production quotas, and regularly agreed to push up prices. If a customer refused to accept the higher prices from their usual suppliers, they were simply quoted even higher prices by other cartel members. The industry claimed in its defence that it was not making money out of the product, and at one time had 50 per cent excess capacity. Although the total fines of £37 million seem huge, and were the largest ever imposed by the Commission, they amounted to less than 0.5 per cent of the companies' turnover. It took a long time to discover the existence of the cartel, and many of its members probably profited from it despite the fine.

The second case concerns seven Belgian firms producing roofing felt. They were fined ECU 1 million (£663,000) by the Commission for forming a cartel in 1978. The agreement was a national one, but was designed to exclude firms from other EC countries. The cartel operated a system of quotas, minimum price lists and action against new members. It did not allow equipment to fall into the hands of non-members of the cartel, and had a system of maximum discounts. Despite the smallness of the companies and the fine itself, it does illustrate the extent to which EC legislation can effect national practices.

The Commission had limited immediate success when it took the restrictive practices of European airlines to the Court of Justice, although it was accepted by the Court that the activities of national airlines were covered by Article 85. Before April 1986, it was argued by the member states that airline cartels were outside the scope of the Treaty. This ruling caused the member states to look carefully at the possibility of liberalising air traffic. Typically, most routes were shared on a bilateral basis, with fares being far in excess of what might have been the case if there had been unrestricted competition. The problem of deregulation was that it posed a threat to the national flag carriers, which were a source of pride, and in many cases were actually owned by the state. Complete deregulation was therefore ruled out on the basis that it attacked national as well as commercial interests, despite the real benefits it could offer the ordinary citizen.

Dominant firms and Article 86

This article concerns itself with the activities of firms who abuse their dominant position in the market. The existence of large firms who dominate markets is not in itself a bad thing. Dominance can come about because of a firm's superior efficiency. Having market power by virtue of being better at producing a particular product, can be of benefit to consumers, and be essential in order to be competitive on a world-wide basis.

Article 86 does not make it clear what it considers a dominant position to be, which is sensible given the difficulty of defining these things. What the article does do, is to set out the kind of practices that a dominant firm should not resort to. Dominant firms should not impose unfair prices or trading conditions on their trading partners. If they use their market power to either exploit or maintain their dominance, they can be prosecuted by the Commission. Unlike Article 85, firms are not expected to report their dominance to the Commission. Prosecutions depend upon either the Commission's investigations, or complaints about firms' activities. Although Article 86 does not mention merger activity as a method of gaining dominance, it would appear that they do fall within the ambit of the Article, in that they may be used to establish dominance.

The Commission has had less success with the problem of dominant firms than it has had with restrictive practices, perhaps because of a lack of resources to investigate these activities thoroughly. A case which attracted a great deal of attention in the late 1970s was that against the Swiss multinational Hoffman-La Roche. The company was the dominant producer of vitamins. In the case of vitamins B_2 and H, their share of the market was 80 per cent. The company used fidelity payments as a means of keeping customer loyalty. If customers bought exclusively from Roche, they could expect better prices than if they only bought a few of their requirements from them. These fidelity payments were not related to the quantity purchased, but to loyalty. This restriction had the effect of excluding competitors who might have been able to offer certain products cheaper. It therefore helped to maintain the company's dominance.

State aids

The granting of state aids can give a substantial competitive advantage to domestic producers, and as a consequence, many are regarded as being compatible with the Common Market. Under Article 92(1), state aids are not permitted if they effect the EC in any way. However, Article 92(2) exempts certain state aids such as those designed for a social purpose. If the state gives schoolchildren free school milk, this would be allowable, providing any supplier within the Community can tender for the contract. Also, aid given to relieve the effects of a natural disaster, or to help areas disadvantaged by geographical division, such as the West German border with the East, is allowed. Although there is no specific heading for regional policy in the Treaty, Article 93(3) does permit aid going to areas of high unemployment or low incomes, providing such aid is not excessive. Finally, Article 93(2)(b) makes it possible to give aid to promote schemes of Community interest. Help given towards a Channel tunnel might well fall under this category. Also under this heading it is possible to give aid to remedy a serious problem for a national economy. So when British Leyland was in considerable difficulties, the UK Government was able to rescue it without being challenged by the Commission.

Member states are supposed to inform the Commission of any aids being given to industry, and these aids must conform to the requirements of the Treaty. If they do not conform, the Commission can issue a decision requiring the member to either amend or abolish the scheme. In theory the aids should be transparent, that is, their effects on industry should be easily understood. In practice, many of the effects of policy are difficult to understand, and states seek to muddy the ground in order to win an advantage.

In the period 1981–84, the number of notifications of state aids to the Commission, amounted to more than 500, more than double that of the previous four years. By 1985, the trend was moving slightly downward, perhaps due to the scrutiny of the Commission deterring the introduction of some schemes. Many countries still break or bend the rules either by not informing the Commission, or by giving the aid first and asking for permission afterwards. At any time, about 40 cases will be subject to detailed investigation by the Commission's 30 investigators into state aids. The number of staff in this area is, however, not nearly adequate for the task which it faces.

7.3 The restructuring of the steel industry

While the ECs competition policy has gone some way towards discouraging cartels and indiscriminate use of state aids, the Community's policy towards the steel industry represents a substantial contrast. Here the Community has involved itself in a detailed way in the restructuring of an industry facing a major crisis, by both coordinating and providing financial aid, and by restricting competition.

Since 1960, the ECs share of world steel production has declined, as Japan and the newly industrialised countries increased capacity. Europe's steel industry still remains largely national in character, with few companies producing in more than one

Table 7.1 Production of crude steel in the EC Ten

Year	Quantity (*million tonnes*)
1961	96
1965	114
1970	138
1974	150
1975	126
1979	141
1980	128
1981	126
1982	111
1983	109
1984	120

Source: Basic Statistics of the Community 23rd edn Eurostat

country. In the UK, France, Italy and Belgium, a significant proportion of the industry is nationalised. Although some modernisation took place in the fat years to 1974, generally costs of production were higher than those in Japan at the time, because of the failure to build really large plants in order to gain economies of scale. The stimulus to change was not as great as it might have been, because of the protective environment in which the industry operated. As Table 7.1 shows, the downturn of the economy as a result of the oil crisis, brought with it a drastic fall in steel production.

The recession reduced the price of steel by between 35 and 45 per cent. In response the Commission introduced voluntary restrictions on production. In 1980 mandatory production quotas were introduced in response to a second bout of recession. Along with this there were attempts to achieve 'recommended' prices, although the success of these was limited. Once demand fell in 1982, so did prices.

The rationale for community restructuring of the steel industry

Community measures to restrict competition were designed to give the industry a breathing-space in order to reduce capacity and return to profitability. There can be no doubt that if adjustment had been left to unregulated international market forces then the process would have been a lot more painful. The demand for steel depends on the demand for the products which use it, it is not a final production good. If steel prices fall, demand tends to be inelastic, that is, the quantity demanded from the whole industry hardly increases at all. On the production side the industry is highly capital intensive, and requires between 70 and 90 per cent usage of capacity to ensure profitability. If demand falls the tendency is for steel producers to cut prices in order to maintain the tonnage going through their plants. If all producers do this, the intense competition results in even the most efficient losing money. Producers frequently just cover their day-to-day costs, without getting any return on their investment. Added to this, because steel plants are frequently located in traditional heavy industrial areas where jobs are scarce, governments feel the need to step in. Survival depends more on the availability of financial resources than of the efficiency of production.

In this situation some control of national aids is as essential as a restructuring programme. The EC needed to close down some of its outdated capacity in order to stay internationally competitive. It also had to adjust to the reality of a generally lower level of output due to some loss of international market share. Added to this there has been a trend towards the replacement of steel by newer materials such as plastics and ceramics, or simply to use less steel to make products like motor cars.

The Community's measures

The legal basis for Community action is based on the Treaty of Paris of 1951, which set up the ECSC. The High Authority of the ECSC (forerunner of the Commission) was given extensive powers to forbid cartels, promote research and development, as well as finance retraining. It also had the power to prohibit excessive investment. With the agreement of the Council it was able to declare a state of 'imminent crisis' and set minimum prices. If conditions in the industry warranted it, it was also possible to declare a state of manifest crisis, in which case production quotas could be imposed. It was not until the mid 1970s that these powers were first used, and in 1980, that a state of manifest crisis was declared.

By the end of 1985, the crisis was thought to be largely over, and the EC prohibited the use of state aids, except for environmental purposes, and the closure of inefficient plants. The industry was still operating at 70 per cent capacity, and it was estimated that 25 million tonnes of capacity needed phasing out. Between 1975 and 1984, 350,000 jobs had been lost in the industry. The social cost of restructuring was therefore very high, but at least the industry was ready to move towards normal trading.

The use of production quotas was generally a success, and the EC's policy for the industry worked well. Future policy does pose a number of problems, in that demand is unlikely to grow significantly. Indeed there are indications that in the late 1980s there is at least 15 million tonnes of spare capacity. This means that future adjustments to get rid of surplus and out-of-date capacity are going to lead to job losses, and perhaps future states of crisis. Quotas are likely to be reduced again, and this implies that national governments are going to face some difficult decisions about plant closures.

Finally, although the EC makes much of its contribution towards the social costs of adjustment, this is a policy which has had little success. Throwing money at areas of high unemployment through retraining schemes does not replace the jobs lost. Inevitably these areas are likely to remain in a depressed state for a long time to come.

7.4 Promoting new technology

There is nothing new about new technology in Europe, or indeed anywhere in the world. Industrial society is in a continuous state of change, although there are periods in which the pace of change is more rapid than others. In the period from 1946 to 1973 high rates of economic growth were achieved relatively easily, helped along by an increased working population and productivity growth. This growth in productivity was achieved by better working methods, a movement of labour into the more productive areas of the economy, increased investment and the adoption of new technology. Since 1973 it has been more difficult to achieve a satisfactory growth rate, and governments have looked for strategies to remedy this stagnation.

As part of their strategy, many governments have attempted to promote new technology by either directly funding research and development (R&D), or indirectly funding it by devices such as public procurement programmes. Added to this, attempts have been made to improve the general environment for developing and adopting new technology. Why should the state be involved in what is often seen as a private sector concern? The main argument is that left to itself the market under-produces in terms of this key element of economic development. Also, the risks involved in spending on R&D for the private sector may be high. Unless new ideas can be adequately protected, and there is sufficient finance to bring them to fruition, firms may stay shy of heavy involvement in these activities. Firms may of course be able to license new patents. Here the Japanese have had great success, but there is a limit to the extent that this free riding can continue. Smaller firms may not have the access to the patents or may be incapable of exploiting them without the help of governments. Domestically based firms may find that they are overwhelmed by large multinational corporations who use new technology as a competitive weapon. These multinationals are able to use their financial power to switch to high growth sectors and maintain their dominance on a world-wide basis.

In 1982 the USA spent $79 billion on R&D, which was about 2.6 per cent of GDP, while the EC Ten spent $53 billion, amounting to 2.2 per cent of GDP, and Japan spent approximately $28 billion, about 2.47 per cent of GDP. The public sector funds about half the R&D in both the EC and the USA. However, 65 per cent of US public spending goes on military-related projects, in comparison to 25 per cent for the EC. In contrast the Japanese state funds only 25 per cent of R&D, with 2 per cent of this being spent on military projects.

In the 1960s the technological gap between Europe and the USA was a source of continuing debate. This was an issue that was largely forgotten about in the 1970s but re- emerged in the 1980s. In particular there was a feeling that Europe was falling behind in the area of high-technology trade, and that this was affecting the growth of the economy. Growth rates in production of high-technology products remained at only 5 per cent per annum in the period 1972–85, compared to 7.6 per cent for the USA and 14 per cent for Japan. In 1983, these products made up only 25 per cent of European exports, which was the same as 20 years before, while it had risen from 25 to 38 per cent for the USA, and from 16 to 42 per cent for Japan. The speed at which the Japanese have been able to dominate is illustrated in the case of semiconductors. In 1980, the USA had 60 per cent of the world market in semiconductors, while Japan had 25 per cent and Europe 13 per cent. By 1985, the USA's share of this market had declined to 47 per cent while the Japanese had gained 39 per cent, and Europe's share had declined to 11 per cent.

Although the pessimism about economic growth rates was justifiable, and European companies have done poorly in the important new technology market, the level of R&D spending could hardly be blamed. There are more than 1 million scientists and technicians in Europe, a third of whom are employed in research work. There can be no doubt about the ability of the Europeans to invent. Despite the success of the USA in areas like semiconductors, the growth of their economy was related more to the ability to generate jobs. It is the Japanese who have gained most from the application of new technology and who have shown the greatest ability to bring it speedily onto the world's markets. It is in the development and production stage that the trade battle is won and lost, and this is one area where Europe is poor. A rough rule of thumb is said to be that for every £1 spent on research, £10 must be spent on development and £100 on production.

European firms, with a lack of a unified market, are at a disadvantage, given that they may be expected to produce for a number of differing standards. National governments tend to make things worse by their insistence on trying to promote a number of national champions, which holds back market forces. The challenge for Europe is to use its resources to the best advantage. If there is excessive competition in R&D, firms may be duplicating basic research. Within the EC, the member states would all benefit from a sharing of information, and a greater degree of specialisation. Each successive stage in developing new technology becomes more expensive, and individual member states may not have the resources to compete adequately. This is especially the case where projects are denied an adequate return on their investment because of the fragmentation of the EC market.

European industry has learned to cooperate on a limited basis by the development of collaborative projects. For example the British and French national electricity grids are linked by a cross-Channel cable in order to pool resources to relieve peak loads. In aircraft production there has been a long, if not always successful, history of collaboration. The most famous example here being the Anglo-French Concorde. A more successful example from a commercial point of view might be the Airbus project which involves the collaboration of Britain with British Aerospace holding a 20 per cent stake, France with Aerospatiale having a 38 per cent stake, West Germany with Deutsche Airbus holding 38 per cent, and finally Spain with CASA owning 4 per cent. The establishment of the Airbus was an attempt to provide a viable alternative to the dominance of the American airframe industry, which in 1978 had something like 90 per cent of the world market. The Airbus project is subsidised by the participating countries, and this has caused the US Government to protest about unfair competition. The validity of this claim is, however, difficult to judge because of the unwillingness of the member governments to release adequate accounts. Estimates as to the extent of state support vary from between $10 billion and $5 billion for the A320 aircraft alone. However, at launch it had 261 orders, and 176 options for sale, which is the best ever in terms of advanced orders. Although the return on the investment may be poor, it is worth remembering that the aircraft does at least provide an alternative to the monopoly power of the American producers. Boeing has had a monopoly on the supply of the very large jets for some time, with its 747, and simply names its price.

There is collaboration in the production of military aircraft, but beyond the area of defence, and state-sponsored prestige projects, the number of examples is limited. In the vital area of information technology, member governments have stuck with promoting national champions or companies have collaborated with predominantly non-European partners. The Unidata scheme launched in 1972, was an attempt by CII of France, Siemens of West Germany and Philips of the Netherlands, to launch a European challenge to the dominance of the American multinational, International Business Machines (IBM). It came to nothing, due to a lack of commitment. As a consequence of these and other companies not working together, industry in the EC has failed to establish an adequate platform to attack the world market and has become vulnerable to imports in those areas where it should perform well.

The Community response

The EC's involvement in scientific activity is a long one, dating back to the ECSC in 1951, and Euratom in 1958. These were, however, raw material and energy related. In 1973, the energy crisis gave an impetus to step up this area of activity. In 1974, it was agreed that the Community should have an involvement in all fields of science and technology apart from those affecting military and industrial secrets, and the Commission was given the task of coordinating national science policies. While these were important developments, real progress was limited until 1979 when Commissioner Davignon got together a working group of the 12 largest electronics companies. These companies along with the Commission were able to develop the European Strategic Programme for Research and Development in Information Technology (ESPRIT). The importance of this industry was becoming apparent in that 5 per cent of Europe's working population was working in the information industry, and it was influencing something between a half and a third of all those who were economically active. Because the newly industrialised countries were overtaking Europe in the traditional industries, it was important to look to growth areas like this. The need for the EC to concentrate on this sector became even more apparent when the Japanese announced their Fifth Generation Computer Program in 1981. Their aim was to obtain 40 per cent of the world computer-related market by 1990.

Of the major EC collaborative projects, ESPRIT was the first, and was all the more important because it was generated by industry rather than by the bureaucrats. It was designed to overcome the fragmentation of the R&D effort in the EC, but was more selective than many national programmes. Its aim was to bring together firms or institutions from more than one EC country. At least 50 per cent of finance was to come from the participating partners, and it was for what was described a 'pre-competitive research'. This meant that much of the results of the work would not be immediately applicable, at least in theory. In practice, however, it seems unlikely that firms would involve themselves in this kind of activity without some thought as to its pay-off, although universities and other non-commercial organisations might. The programme started in December 1982 with a pilot scheme where 38 projects were launched. These were incorporated into the main programme when it got under way in 1984; ESPRIT was designed to be in two five-year phases, the first being given ECU 750 million. It covered advanced micro-electronic capability, software technology, advanced information processing, office systems and computer-integrated manufacture.

The best feature of ESPRIT is that it has promoted cooperation between firms, which is something that has not happened in the past. It has meant that firms have looked for partners within Europe instead of seeking them in the USA or in Japan. It has been the subject of some criticism, however. First because it is difficult for small firms to participate, although they have not been excluded. However, in an industry which is dominated by large firms, it is to be expected that small firms will find it difficult to participate. Second, there was the suggestion that non-European firms might benefit from the basic research. However, such firms must have substantial European research facilities if they are to participate in the scheme. In that case there are likely to be advantages for the EC as well. The major criticism is that the ECU 750 million over five years, is simply not sufficient to make the kind of impact that is required. It compares poorly with the \$2 billion or more per year being spent by the largest American companies on research in this area, and is a fraction of the money being devoted to even the smallest parts of the CAP.

Despite being rather late in the day to launch this kind of initiative, the ESPRIT programme has been seen as a big success, and now serves as a model for other schemes. The basis of this evaluation is perhaps more political than scientific, because up to the end of 1986, ESPRIT had failed to produce any major breakthrough. An example of a programme based on ESPRIT, is the R&D in Advanced Communication Technology for Europe (RACE) programme which had its initial phase from 1985 to 1986, and was designed to help the EC remain in the forefront of the telecommunications industry. Also, there is the Basic Research in Industrial Technology for Europe (BRITE) programme, a four-year programme running from 1985 to 1988, which aims to encourage the development and spread of new technologies to the traditional industries, which still account for three-quarters of industrial employment. In the future, it would seem that still more schemes will be generated. This means that more generous long-term finance for projects is essential. If schemes are to be a success, it is clear that there must be a move towards more commercially based research, with more companies involved.

It would appear that the EC has now taken the view that it has a responsibility for correcting some of the market failures in the field of new technology. The commitment to this task is such that the Single European Act, states that: 'The Community's aim shall be to strengthen the scientific and technological basis of European industry and to encourage it to become more competitive at an international level.'[1] In particular, emphasis in the Act is placed upon common research and technological development, and the need to develop the internal market.

7.5 Conclusion

The EC has moved some way in its attitude towards industry. It no longer sees its role as being limited to preventing restrictive practices, and helping declining heavy industries to adapt, although these are still important functions. It now rightly sees that it has an important role to play in promoting change, either by developing the internal market or by promoting R&D. It would be a mistake to expect too much from collaborative schemes, however, unless the Community can devise methods of translating the success of research into viable commercial products. Also, there is a real danger that collaboration will result in weak national champions being replaced by European champions who rely on subsidies or protection to survive.

7.6 References

1. Commission of the EC 1986 Single European Act, Article 130 F.

Chapter eight

The Common Agricultural Policy – a case for urgent reform

In most advanced economies the agricultural industry is subject to considerable government intervention. Within the EC, the CAP aims to support agriculture on a Community-wide basis, thus replacing national policies, in an attempt to ensure a balance of benefits to both producers and consumers. It is regarded as the most developed Communities policy and covers over 90 per cent of agricultural products; and yet there are constant calls for very fundamental reform. The major reasons for these demands are:

1. Agricultural prices are high, which stimulates uneconomic production and disadvantages the consumer.
2. The budgetary cost of the CAP. It absorbs in excess of two-thirds of the EC's budget, and as a consequence starves other policy areas of adequate funding.
3. The pricing system results in substantial resource transfers which can be attributed to the CAP, but do not show up in the budget. Food-importing countries within the EC have to pay higher than world market prices for food, while surplus producers gain privileged access to these markets.
4. Surpluses are dumped on world markets. These disturb the markets for other agricultural exporters without benefiting the EC's consumers.
5. Little emphasis is placed upon the environmental aspects of agricultural policy.

These criticisms are particularly relevant to the UK which has only 2.5 per cent of its working population employed in the agricultural industry compared to a Community average of 7.7 per cent. Also, despite substantial gains in productivity, the UK still only produces 60 per cent of its requirements and is a major food importer.

8.1 The rationale for agricultural support

Agriculture is an industry which does not function well in a free-market environment. Demand tends to be price inelastic, and in the short term supply is also price inelastic. Actual supply may, however, vary by as much as 25 per cent due to factors such as climate and the existence of pests and disease. The fluctuations in supply, plus a lack of market knowledge, means that agricultural markets may behave erratically. That is, farmers are small producers, compared with the size of the market, and are as a consequence, price takers. They tend to respond to market signals without realising their true significance, so they produce more in response to price changes, rather than responding to actual demand changes.

This can be partly explained by economic theory through the use of the cobweb theorem, also known by its appropriate picturesque nickname of the 'Hog Cycle'. In agriculture there is frequently a supply lag of over a year, so that if prices rise, supply does not respond for some time. (In the case of pigs, the lag used to be two or three years.) This means that shortages are not readily accommodated for in the short term; however, a period of high prices may bring about an exaggerated response from producers in the future. The result is a glut of the product and a period of low prices. Fig. 8.1 illustrates the process.

If there is a shortage this year, supply will be at A, and that will mean that prices will rise to B. Because supply cannot be increased in the short term, prices will stay high for some time. The period of high prices will, after a delay, produce increased supply, but at a level C that corresponds to the high prices. Production will now be too high, and a glut will result in prices falling to D. The equi-

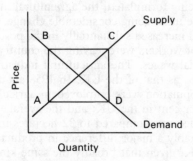

Fig. 8.1 The cobweb

librium between supply and demand is never reached, and agricultural markets will lurch between shortage and glut.

Added to these problems, there may be periods of over-supply which are general and long term. Rural incomes will be depressed, and this may cause migration from the countryside to the cities. This is a particular problem for developed nations, where better technology has led to increased productivity in farming. Even in times of economic expansion, however, the demand for food does not tend to rise as rapidly as incomes. This is because consumers do not simply eat more because they are better off. Typically, the UK has an income elasticity of demand for food of 0.14, although it is considerably higher for individual products such as cream where it is about 0.90. These are problems of the domestic markets, where again there are periods of shortage and surplus.

In theory, a great deal could be done to stabilise markets by better market information. The majority of states do not take this view, however, and they attempt to stabilise the industry by either physical controls or by supporting the market process. The fact that governments are intervening in the market mechanism means that the area becomes politicised. It gives scope for governments to determine prices and incomes in the industry and encourage production. The method and extent of intervention will depend on the strategic role of the industry. This will be influenced by factors such as the size and structure of the industry, the importance of food supplies and the contribution to the balance of payments. Other factors will also be important such as the value placed upon the rural way of life.

8.2   The development of the CAP

At the time the CAP was being formulated, the agricultural industries of the original Six were undergoing considerable change. The degree of mechanisation had increased substantially in the post-war period and large numbers of workers were leaving the countryside attracted by higher industrial wages. The agricultural industry of the Six was not as developed as that of the UK. In 1958 about 20 per cent of the working population were employed in agriculture in the Six compared to 5 per cent in the UK; and the average size of holdings was only 10.4 hectares compared to 32 hectares in the UK. The result was predictably a major difference in productivity between the Six and the UK, given that broadly the same kind of crops were being produced. The difference in the size of the holdings still exists today, as the average size in the Ten is 15.7 hectares compared with 68.7 hectares for the UK.

The reason for the superior structure of UK agriculture is largely historical. The system of inheritance in the UK had always encouraged the consolidation of holdings, while in countries like France, holdings were often split on the death of the landowner. Added to this, factors such as greater exposure to international competition helped to spur on change in the UK, while continental producers were often protected by tariff walls.

The general objectives of the CAP are those set out in Article 39 of the Treaty of Rome. They would be broadly acceptable to almost any country within Western Europe, and are as follows:

1. To increase agricultural productivity by promoting technical progress and by ensuring the rational development of agricultural production and the optimum utilisation of the factors of production, in particular labour.
2. To ensure a fair standard of living for the agricultural community, in particular by increasing the individual earnings of persons engaged in agriculture.
3. To stabilise markets.
4. To guarantee the availability of supplies.
5. To ensure reasonable consumer prices.

It took 10 years of negotiation to translate these objectives into a workable policy, and get rid of much of the national price support mechanism, so that it was not until 1968 that the CAP could be regarded as established.

Prior to the formation of the EC all the Six had farm policies which contained varying degrees of protection. In order to gain agreement, the overall level of protection from imports was increased. In the early years, there were no significant surpluses, so that it was the consumer, not the taxpayer, who paid. This redistribution could be justified to some extent, because the economies of the Six were growing rapidly.

In contrast, the system of support for agriculture in the UK was traditionally based upon the concept of cheap food. The primary method of support was deficiency payments. This involved paying farmers subsidies so that they could compete with cheaper imports, and had the effect of encouraging production at the taxpayers' expense. It was feasible because the UK industry was relatively small and efficient. However, by the 1960s, as agricultural productivity rose and world prices fell, the system became an increasing burden on the taxpayer. Attempts were then made to control the cost of subsidies by raising import prices; so that at the time of UK accession the two systems were, to a limited extent, starting to converge.

By the late 1960s two major problems concerning the CAP started to emerge. The first was that of surplus production, and its related budgetary costs. The second was the divergence of exchange rates, which meant the EC was a very long way from enjoying common prices. Both these problems remain with us and will be dealt with later in the chapter.

8.3 Operating the CAP

The operation of the CAP is designed around three main principles:

1. Community preference against imports.
2. Community free trade.
3. Shared financial responsibility.

The responsibility for financing price support and structural change is vested in the European Agricultural Guarantee and Guidance Fund (EAGGF), which typically takes an alarming 70 per cent of the EC's total budget. The guarantee element predominates, normally taking 95 per cent of funds for price support, while only around 5 per cent is spent on the guidance section. Most guidance payments are made to member states, in the form of refunds for spending on structural improvements and aid to less favoured areas.

Fixing prices

The CAP major characteristic is its system of support for market prices in order to maintain farm incomes, although the use of quotas to control surplus production is likely to be of increasing importance. The fixing of Community-wide prices is essentially a political decision undertaken annually. The process is complex because of the need to balance the variety of national interest with budgetary constraints. Because of the diversity of European agriculture, it is impossible to fix a Community price which takes account of differing levels of farm productivity, maintains comparable farm incomes and takes account of the need to balance supply and demand. The huge differences in productivity levels between member states is illustrated in Table 8.1. It should be remembered

Table 8.1 Divergence within the CAP

| | Average yields (tonnes per hectare) | | | |
Crop	Portugal 1982	Spain 1983	UK 1983	Denmark 1983
Wheat	1.2	2.5	7.6	7.2
Oats	0.5	1.7	5.1	4.8
Barley	0.7	2.7	5.5	5.2

Source: Financial Times, 23 December 1985

that some individual producers will be more or less efficient than these figures suggest.

In the past, the dilemma was resolved by fixing the prices at high enough levels to maintain the incomes of the less productive. As a consequence, efficient producers gained excessive returns and production was encouraged, leading to surpluses. Not surprisingly, the budgetary crisis that the EC faces makes this kind of solution less attractive. Within the system of supposedly uniform prices, national price changes still take place, although with the Commission's approval. This occurs via the system of green currencies which has become an established part of the CAP.

Mechanism for price support

There are a variety of methods of price support which apply to products covered by the CAP. While it would seem natural to set CAP prices in ECUs, from 1984 it was agreed to use the strongest currency in the EMS, the West German mark. As an illustration of how it works we can examine one product – common wheat. There are three Community-wide prices in operation:

1. *Target price*. This is based upon grain prices delivered into store at Duisburg, the place in the Community where grain is in shortest supply. The price for other areas is calculated by allowing for transport costs. This is the price fixed by the Council of Ministers and is the basis for the other prices. In theory it is the ideal price for the Community. In practice, however, because of over-production within the Community, it has ceased to be meaningful unless there is a world-wide shortage.

2. *Threshold price*. This is the price that imports of grain come into the EC. It is set at a similar level to the target price. The

aim is to ensure that imported grain does not flood into the EC. A tax called a variable levy is placed upon imported grain. It is calculated on a daily basis by taking the difference between the lowest world market price (delivered to the EC) and the threshold price. So the variable levy goes up when world prices fall, and vice versa. The price moves up over the season to encourage orderly marketing. In the unlikely event of world prices being above the EC price, a variable tax is placed upon exports from the EC in the hope that prices within the Community will not rise above target price.

3. *Intervention price.* This is the theoretical minimum price for grain within the Community, although in practice farmers are likely to get paid less because of:
   (a) delivery and handling costs;
   (b) delayed payments – in order to encourage sellers to find alternative markets, payment is not made for three months after being sold into intervention.

The intervention mechanism operates by grain being withdrawn from the market either by taking it into store, or by subsidies being paid to traders to export onto the world market. The Community spends about twice as much on export subsidies as on storage. Traders have to tender for the subsidy (refunds) which they only receive after proof that the grain has been exported. As with the threshold price, intervention prices move up over the season to encourage orderly marketing.

The effects of the intervention system on the grain market can be illustrated by Fig. 8.2.

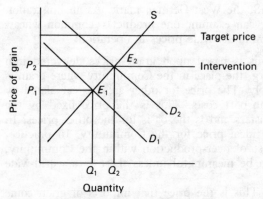

Fig. 8.2 The intervention mechanism

Left to itself, the market equilibrium is at E_1 which is below intervention price. As grain is purchased, the demand curve shifts from D_1 to D_2 which gives a new equilibrium point E_2. Prices rise from P_1 to P_2 which is the intervention price. The farmer can rely on a stable price for his grain, but the disadvantage for the Community is that prices are constantly fixed above the level where demand equals supply. The farmer can produce as much as he wishes, regardless of the fact that there is surplus production.

Green money

The early development of the CAP took place in an era of low inflation and monetary stability. As a consequence, the aim of creating a common price structure for agricultural products looked realistic. However, by the late 1960s, just as the broad framework of the CAP had been agreed, the Bretton Woods system of fixed exchange rates started to come apart. In 1967, the British pound was devalued; this was followed in 1969 by the devaluation of the French franc and the revaluation of the German mark. The early 1970s then saw inflation rates increase dramatically throughout the world and the replacement of fixed exchange rates by floating exchange rates.

The implication for the CAP of the new era of floating exchange rates was that the system of common prices was supplemented by the introduction of green rates (representative rates). This was done initially to protect national economies from some of the effects of abrupt price changes due to movements in the exchange rate. Later, as floating exchange rates became an established feature, it also developed into an instrument of national farm policy.

Prior to the introduction of green rates, agricultural prices were set in UAs which were the same rate as the US dollar. National prices were calculated simply by fixed exchange rates. The problem arose in 1969 when the French franc was devalued, because prices fixed in Brussels should have applied to the French economy. Being fixed externally, the result of the devaluation would have been that farm prices would rise. This would not only be inflationary, but also have rewarded farmers unjustly. In the case of the German revaluation, the effect of externally fixed agricultural prices would have meant farm prices falling. Although this would have benefited consumers, the West German farmers would have suffered. The decision was made, therefore, to keep prices within the two countries the same in terms of national currencies. This can be best explained by the following hypothetical examples:

1. Original exchange rate 1 UA = 5 DM = 10 Fr.f.
2. If 1 tonne of wheat is priced at 10 UA, its price in West Germany would be 50 marks and in France 100 francs.
3. If the mark is revalued by 10 per cent and the franc devalued by 10 per cent, the new exchange rate would be 1 UA = 4.5 DM = 11 Fr.f.
4. Without green rates, our tonne of wheat would, after currency movements, be still priced at 10 UAs, but in West Germany prices would fall to 45 marks per tonne and in France prices rise to 110 francs per tonne.
5. With green rates, prices diverge as illustrated, even though they stay the same in national currencies. So national producers still receive the same price as before the currency movement. The effects of a currency devaluation on a common price are shown in Fig. 8.3.

The green rates could not work without additional intervention to stop grain moving from the lowest-priced markets to the highest-priced markets. In order to stop this a system of subsidies and taxes called Monetary Compensatory Amounts (MCAs) was introduced. In our example, exports to France from another community country would benefit from a subsidy paid by the EAGGF. In the case of West Germany, border taxes on imports would be charged in order to maintain the higher prices.

Monetary Compensatory Amounts can only be changed by the unanimous agreement of all member states, and this is normally done as part of the annual price review. They are designed to prevent the distortion effect of green currencies.

Positive MCAs allow high prices within a country to be maintained by means of a tax on imports. Exports from that country

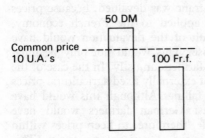

Fig. 8.3 The effect of currency devaluation

will have to be subsidised. The producers will benefit, but at the expense of the consumer.

Negative MCAs keep prices low within a country by subsidising imports. Exports to the rest of the Community will be taxed.

National prices

Over the years the green money system has developed considerably, so that it is now used as a tool of national policy. By devaluing the green rates, it is possible to raise prices to farmers, and, of course, revaluation would lower them. Although the UK operates with a single green rate, France operates with five rates, so it is possible in their case to differentiate between products.

The case for the green rates system is that it permits agricultural prices to reflect the needs of the country concerned. They are regarded as essential given the absence of monetary stability, although there may be a case for relating them more closely to purchasing power parity. This, as a compromise, would at least ensure that changes were not as dramatic as those of market rates of exchange.

The Commission is against green rates remaining in the long term, and supports the EMS as a way of resolving the problems of monetary instability within the community. Green rates mean that the principle of free trade is violated. Apart from this, they cause the transfer of resources from those countries with negative MCAs to those with positive MCAs. Finally, MCAs have an affect on both production and consumption. If national prices are fixed too high, production may be encouraged, and consumption levels may fall, or change between commodities.

In 1984, the EC took steps to try and eliminate MCAs by calculating them on the basis of the currency which revalued most within the EMS. This mechanism was introduced for a three-year period, and had the effect of eliminating the need for positive MCAs. The hope was that negative MCAs would be eliminated as soon as possible after that date. The experiment meant that in practice pricing was in West German marks, but this caused problems, because when there was a change in the parities in the EMS, it gave a windfall price increase to the farmers in countries which did not revalue. The result of currency movements over a period of time are illustrated by the situation in early 1987, where UK farmers were receiving £112 per tonne for their wheat, while those in West Germany were paid £150 per tonne and those in France recived £140 per tonne.

The growing crisis of over-production and price support

The CAP system of price support had the effect of offering, for most products, the guarantee of an unlimited market at a certain price. This incentive, coupled with improved technology, meant that agricultural production in the EC increased dramatically. In the first 20 years of the CAP, agricultural production increased, on average, at about 2.5 per cent per year, despite 10 million workers leaving the land. Consumption has increased by only 0.5 per cent per year, so almost inevitably the EC has moved into a crisis of over-production. The CAP was devised when EC agricultural markets were either in balance or in deficit, so the system provided no mechanism for adequate control of production.

At the time of UK membership, the crisis was masked to a certain extent by a world commodity boom, and the fact that the UK was a major food importer. However, as world prices fell, and UK production increased along with the rest of the EC countries, the cost of the CAP escalated out of control, with disposal costs of some products amounting to some 80 per cent of their value. Given the catching-up process among many of the backward agricultural producers, the trend towards increased productivity looks like making matters worse. Developments like the increased exploitation of Friesian cows would have been welcomed in the past. They are now regarded as something to be actively discouraged, because their ability to produce high milk yields will simply add to the problem of surpluses.

The stimulus which price support gives to increased production has caused a number of related problems to occur. Large-scale producers of cereals see that hedgerows do not give a sufficient return, and have turned parts of the rural landscape into prairies. At the same time, the frequent use of chemicals to stimulate food production brings into question the purity of the food we eat.

Finally, price support has failed to give the kind of social equality that some desired from the policy. The CAP favours certain products which are produced in greater quantities in better-off areas. Also, in many cases, the structure of farming is better in these areas.

The cost of the CAP

Surprisingly, little is known about the burden the CAP places upon the citizens of Europe, despite the continuous clamour for the budgetary cost to be brought under control. The costs are wide-spread, and include:

1. The budgetary cost of market support including export sub-sidies and storage costs.
2. Payments made by the guidance section of the EAGGF towards structural improvements in the industry and to help disadvantaged areas.
3. National governments, budgetary support for research, infra-structure and advisory services.
4. Transfers from consumers via higher prices being paid for food within the EC.

The extent to which the cost of this last item can be calculated, depends upon the ability of economists to estimate what world prices would be if they were not depressed by the dumping of CAP surpluses on to non-EC markets. A study by the Australian Bureau of Agricultural Economics in 1985 suggested that CAP surpluses depressed wheat, meat and sugar prices between 9 and 17 per cent, while those of butter were depressed by 28 per cent. The study estimates that support of one type or another amounts to something like 60 per cent of the value added by the industry i.e. the gross value of production minus inputs such as fertilisers. The largest element of support is the transfer from consumers via higher prices. This element reached its peak in 1977–78, but has declined as a proportion subsequently, as more has had to be spent on subsidising exports. The total cost of transfers to EC agriculture varied from ECU 57 billion to ECU 73 billion between 1976 and 1984 (using 1984 prices) with each non-farm consumer paying ECU 245 per year.

The costs and benefits of the policy are not distributed evenly. The top 25 per cent of farms by size, gain something like 75 per cent of budgetary support, averaging ECU 9,700 per farm each year. The remaining farmers attract only an average of ECU 1,000 per farm each year.

British agriculture has generally prospered under the CAP because of its structure, with a high percentage of larger farms. In contrast, the citizen has done badly because the UK is a major food importer and is obliged to purchase the shortfall in domestic supplies from the expensive Community source, rather than the cheaper world market. As a consequence, the resource transfer from the UK to the Community is far greater than is indicated in the budget. Even within the country, the policy affects citizens unevenly. In the UK the poorest 20 per cent of the population spend 25 per cent of their income on food, while the top 20 per cent, spend only 18 per cent.

Those countries who enjoy a comparative advantage in food production find the action of groups like the EC particularly irritating. They find that markets are destabilised, and there is a constant risk of price wars breaking out. This, in turn, may put greater pressure on the CAP. The USA, as a major world producer of food, has got the power to match the CAP, and it is estimated by the Commission that every 10 per cent depreciation of the dollar, relative to the ECU will add between ECU 7 billion and ECU 10 billion to the EC budget. It is not only in the agricultural sector that the effects of the CAP are felt, however, as the dispute between the EC and the USA concerning maize exports to Spain in 1986 was to show. This dispute, was resolved only in January 1987, after the threat of a full-scale trade war breaking out. If this had developed, then all sectors of the economy would have to pay the price of protectionism within the CAP.

Reforming the CAP

The CAP has survived into the 1980s with its price support mechanism largely intact, despite floating exchange rates and mounting surpluses. Most radical proposals for reform have simply come to nothing because of an absence of political will.

As early as 1969 the EC was making incentive payments to destroy milking cows and convert to beef production. In 1976 sugar quotas were introduced and in 1977 co-responsibility payments were introduced for milk. These are a means whereby producers share in the cost of disposal of surpluses by a levy on production. Generally the EC has adopted a policy of disposal of surplus production. Internally, this has been done by schemes like the Christmas butter promotion; however, this sort of policy is most useful as a propaganda exercise. The normal route of disposal has been via exports. That is, the EC has dumped surplus production on world markets, so helping to destabilise them, and add the charge of unfair competition to that of domestic protectionism.

These kind of policies have done little to change the basic market signals which are the cause of the over-production problem. The difficulty is, that substantial price reductions would be required to bring markets back into equilibrium. As Table 8.2 illustrates, the demand for most kinds of food is inelastic.

By the early 1980s the forces for changing the CAP were growing more intense. Most immediately, something would have to be

Table 8.2 Price elasticities of some agricultural products in the UK in 1976

Liquid milk	−0.18
Cheese	−0.11
Butter	−0.30
Eggs	−0.11
Sugar	−0.47
All meat	−0.99
Fresh potatoes	−0.17
Fresh green vegetables	−0.15 to −3.60
Apples	−0.64
Pears	−1.71

Source: Hill and Ingersent 1982 p 83

done, simply because the EC was running out of money. There were problems associated with the further enlargement of the EC to the south. Added to this, the economic downturn made many question why agriculture needed pampering when industry was suffering so badly.

In 1980, the Commission made a number of radical suggestions to cope with the crisis in the CAP. These included narrowing the gap between EC and world market prices, no longer giving full support for products in surplus, and the introduction of production targets. Added to these, other suggestions have been made, for example, direct income support to farmers and very much more active structural policies geared to the region.

In 1984, milk quotas were introduced with some success. Quotas are not an ideal solution in all cases, so in 1985, the Commission once again proposed price reductions as a method of reducing the surplus of cereals within the EC. As is the nature of things within the CAP, suggested reforms often remain just that, without any real action being taken. This was the case once again, and despite an ever-increasing surplus, the best agreement that could be obtained was the introduction of higher quality standards, higher co-responsibility payments and delays in the payment of deliveries into intervention.

In early 1986, some minor price cuts were agreed, but the fear of hostility from farm groups led the West German Government to compensate farmers by national schemes. As a compensation, West German farmers got in excess of £300 million in new subsidies, which encouraged production to stay at previous levels. In other countries, the use of green rates had a similar effect. It was not until a major budget crisis emerged that attempts were made to control production by significant cuts, with a reduction of 13 per cent in the price paid for beef into intervention. Even this was moderated by the effects of the revaluation of the German mark, which gave a price increase to most Community members.

The case of milk quotas

In 1983, milk products took 30.4 per cent of the EAGGF's guarantee section, which is a clear indication of the drain that was on the EC's budget. Fig. 8.4 below shows how production and consumption had diverged.

With production predicted to grow at 3 per cent per annum, it was clear that urgent action needed to be taken. It was calculated by the Commission that a price reduction of 12–13 per cent was required to make any impact on production. This was unaccept-

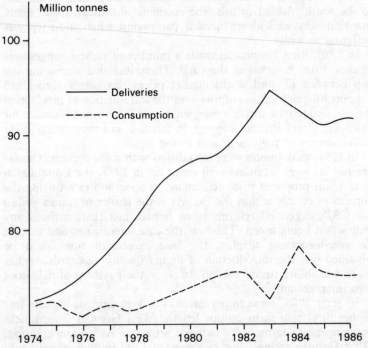

Fig. 8.4 Milk deliveries and consumption in the EC Ten

Source: Commission of the EC *The Situation in the Agricultural Markets 1986*

able, so in order to overcome the problem the EC agreed in April 1984 to the introduction of milk quotas which would apply immediately. The system was to run for five years, with a review after three years. On 14 April 1984 it was decided to base the quota for UK farmers on an output for 1983 less 9 per cent. The intention was to cut production by 6 per cent and allow 3 per cent to cover special cases, for example for farmers who had been out of production temporarily for that year. Excess production was to be subjected to a super-levy, but only if the marketing boards' quota has been exceeded. The penalty was 17.5p per litre of over-production, which is 3p more than the milk was worth. If individual farmers over-produced, they might well have found that because of under-production elsewhere in the area, they did not pay anything.

The operation of quotas can be illustrated diagrammatically in Fig. 8.5: Q_3 is the level of production before quotas are introduced, and Q_2 is the level after quotas. In this situation there is still surplus production, the gap between Q_1 consumer demand, and Q_2 the new level of production. The level of export subsidy required to dispose of surplus production would be the gap between P_1 and P_2. The EC would still have to finance exports to the extent of the shaded area ABCD, but this is an improvement on the situation before quotas when the cost was ACEF.

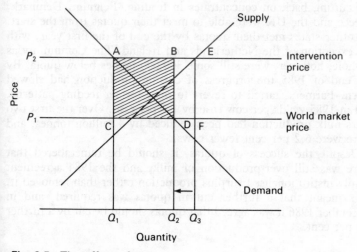

Fig. 8.5 The effect of quotas

Source: Hill 1984

The introduction of quotas was so sudden that many farmers had no time to adjust production in a considered way. Not unnaturally the milk producers protested on the following grounds:

1. Quotas have the effect of reducing output and as a consequence may reduce the utilisation of expensive equipment. This can only be resolved by a system of hiring quotas or buying them, which allows for the shortfall in quota to be made up by others leaving dairying, selling their quotas. This would allow farmers to operate at an efficient level.

2. Land without a quota becomes very much less valuable, so that the quota becomes a major element in land prices.

3. Unless prices are increased, the loss of income may well drive some producers from the land. This is an unfortunate consequence at a time of high unemployment.

4. With an across-the-board quota, the people who did most to cause the surplus have got the largest quotas.

The result of imposing quotas has been generally encouraging in that the production of milk did decline, although at the expense of some farmers who found that their business was no longer viable. By the end of 1984, the number of cows within the Community declined by 3.4 per cent, partly encouraged by national incentives to leave dairying. The average yield per cow was down by 2 per cent, partly due to climatic conditions, but also due to the cutting back on concentrates in feeding. Belgium, Denmark, Greece and the UK were able to meet their quotas from the start. All other states met their quotas by the end of the first year, with the exception of the Netherlands and Ireland. The Community as a whole, however, were still some 300,000 tonnes below quota. By the end of 1985 the progress of cutting production had slowed down. Farmers started to revert to their former feeding patterns, and in 1985 yields per cow rose by 1.7 per cent. Over the first two years milk production had been reduced by 4 million tonnes, and there were 6.2 per cent fewer cows.

Despite the success of quotas, it should be remembered that there was still over-production of milk, and the 1984 agreement simply institutionalised surplus production rather than removed it. This meant that a further cut in quotas was required, and in December 1986 it was agreed that quotas should be cut by a further 9.5 per cent.

8.4 Conclusion

It is clear that there is an urgent need to reform the CAP in such a way as to ensure that large numbers of workers do not leave the land. Firstly, because it costs about four times as much to keep a worker unemployed in the city as against working on the land. Secondly, because depopulation destroys communities and several of the aspects of rural life which many regard as important. At the same time, the folly of massive surpluses in production should be avoided. The broader rural environment must also be considered, as must the potential impact of a larger EC. The use of production quotas in the light of these problems, look inadequate. Perhaps it is now time to modify the price support system severely and move towards a system of income support, preferably financed by national governments. In this way, farmers would be paid as custodians of the countryside and hopefully the CAP would be less burdensome.

With a greater emphasis on the rural way of life, more effort could be put into complementary activities such as developing the countryside for leisure, and the production of handicrafts. Finally, greater emphasis could be placed on the quality of food production, if economies grow the demand for 'naturally produced' foods looks likely to continue.

Chapter nine

The Common Fisheries Policy – a policy success

Fishing is an unusual activity in the modern economy because it is one of man's few remaining commercial hunting activities. In the past the sea's fish were regarded as inexhaustible and available to be exploited by all. Due to modern technology, however, man found ways of increasing catches, and this inevitably led to a resource crisis. The obvious response was to attempt to control catching effort. The fact that fish move around the ocean, often breeding in one place and maturing in another, means that control is best exercised on an international basis. Fisheries would therefore appear to be one of the most promising areas for the EC policy makers. However, the process of developing the policy proved particularly difficult. It took 13 years for a stable and comprehensive regime to materialise. The reasons for this, as we shall see, are a combination of national sentiment, the pursuit of national interest and a basic distrust of international organisations in the area of fishing.

After many years of controversy, the CFP is now in place and is one of the most complete of the EC's policy areas. It has had some success in its attempts to ensure that fish stocks are exploited in a rational way, while protecting the interests of fishermen. This has been done by imposing quotas on catches, providing cash for adjusting fleet sizes and introducing a Community marketing policy. It has gone a long way towards replacing national policies, although agreement covering the Mediterranean area has proved particularly difficult to negotiate, because of the complex political relations between the surrounding states. There are also problems remaining within the policy, for example excess catching capacity, illegal fishing and absorbing the very large Spanish fleet.

9.1 The rationale for a fisheries policy

In the post-Second World War period, not only was the scale of fishing operations increased, but it was combined with improved technology, for example fish-finding equipment, better winding gear, improved net design and the use of factory ships. Nations saw fish as a useful supplement to human diets, and also recognised that it had industrial uses for animal food and fertilisers. The industry was encouraged to such an extent that some fish stocks started to collapse. There were isolated examples of overfishing dating back to the nineteenth century; however, by the 1960s the problem was widespread. As a consequence, within Western Europe, some types of herring had started to disappear, as illustrated in Table 9.1.

A decline in supply need not of course make an industry unprofitable if demand is inelastic or demand is increasing. Indeed, falling catches might even stimulate investment because the product is more valuable. Although the increased catching may not seem sensible from the point of view of the individual fisherman or nation state, it could appear perfectly logical if there is a free for all. With no agreed rules of management, anyone increasing catches does it largely at everyone else's expense. If any individual decides to control catch levels, the existence of 'free riders' means that the sacrifice merely benefits others. The answer therefore must be some kind of collective management of the resource which offers tangible benefits to those who participate in conservation.

Any collective action must take account of biological constraints. The basis of most modern discussion of fisheries economics concerns the model in Fig. 9.1 which sets out some of the broad objectives of fisheries policy.

This simple model suggests possible targets. They do not, of course, take into account social and regional considerations, which can be very important for isolated communities totally dependent on fishing.

Table 9.1 Adult Atlanto – Scandian herring (Norwegian spring spawners catches (000's tons))

Year	1963	1964	1965	1966	1967	1968	1969	1970
Catch	671	1,118	1,326	1,724	1,132	273	24	21

Source: International Council for the Exploration of the Seas, *Comparative Research Report*, No. 37 1974

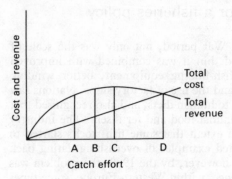

Fig. 9.1 Objectives of fisheries policy

Point A. This is the profit maximisation position, with the greatest gap between total cost and total revenue.

Point B. This is the suggested optimum sustainable yield (OSY). This allows for a margin for error.

Point C. This is the maximum sustainable yield (MSY). Beyond this point any increased fishing simply reduces stocks, and less is available for the future.

Point D. This is the point that the industry would operate at if there was no regulation.

Apart from man's activities, other factors such as disease affect fish stocks, so that biological estimates can never be exact. This has led to a consensus that the most desirable objective is OSY because it allows a margin of error. The problem is that there is no exact agreement where it is, except that it lies to the left of MSY.

The lack of scientific certainty has, in the past, been exploited by non-conservation-minded states to justify fishing in excess of the MSY. The objective of OSY can, therefore, never be realistically achieved unless there is an agreement about resource management and its enforcement. This implies that the concept of free access must be abandoned. Finally, adjusting fleet sizes and social considerations means that, unless stocks are near to collapse, there must be time to adjust.

9.2 Failed attempts at international cooperation

In order to achieve any kind of fisheries policy with objectives not compatible with open exploitation, there must be an effective method of imposing controls on catching effort. Attempts were made to do this by international cooperation. Most notable within European waters was an organisation called the North East Atlantic Fishing Commission (NEAFC). This had a wide membership, including Eastern European states. Typically, NEAFC ignored scientific advice in setting total allowable catches (TACs), because it wished to accommodate all claims to stocks in order to gain agreement. Added to this, the will to enforce agreements did not exist. An example of NEAFC's inability to act was its failure to close down herring fishing, despite the depletion of the Atlanto-Scandian stock. Only in the 1970s did it introduce closed seasons, but these simply resulted in increased fishing for the rest of the year. The failure of NEAFC, and other similar organisations, was caused by the following factors:

1. It had no real control over stocks. The fish existed in the high seas or within national territorial waters.
2. There was no source of pressure to encourage a realistic agreement.
3. Sanctions could not be easily imposed.

In the late 1970s NEAFC was disbanded, only to be resurrected in the early 1980s as a forum for consultation.

9.3 Extending fisheries limits

Until the 1950s the seas were largely free for all, with only three-mile limits being in force. This allowed the development of distant-water fleets which could exploit fishing grounds far away from home. The pressure on fish stocks helped to bring about rapid changes in the international law of the sea, and we are now in a position where 200-mile Exclusive Economic Zones (EEZs) predominate. The sovereign states have the right to exploit the resources within the EEZs. What is left outside these areas, about two-thirds of the world's oceans, is of relatively minor importance, given that fish stocks tend to be concentrated on the continental shelves, which are generally within 200-mile limits. The 200-mile limit meant that the effective jurisdiction of states with long coast-lines has increased dramatically. In the case of Iceland, the extension to 200 miles was the final stage of a thirtyfold increase in the area under its control.

Not surprisingly, these developments caused conflict as they tended to be in advance of international law. It was not until the early 1980s that the third United Nations Conference on the Law of the Sea (UNCLOS III) formally agreed to 200-mile EEZs, and yet they were firmly part of the scene by 1977, the year that the EEC members extended their limits.

The enclosure of much of the world's fishing grounds had three important consequences:

1. Some countries became net beneficiaries in terms of the areas they could fish without competition, while others lost out by being excluded.
2. It led to the displacement of many of the distant-water fleets from what had become their traditional fishing grounds.
3. It gave the opportunity for firmer control over fisheries. In most cases control based on ownership was the only realistic alternative to the failed attempts at cooperation.

All the above points had implications for the CFP, in particular the displacement of distant-water fleets meant that some compensation was sought in domestic waters. The UK distant-water fleet had caught 239,634 tonnes in 1974, or about a quarter of the national catch. By 1981, catches by this part of the fleet were down to 10,726 tonnes. The distant-water vessels largely waited to be scrapped or did other work as they were not suitable for domestic operations. Their decline was not attributable to the EC, yet it did sour relations with the UK demands for compensation. The nationalisation of fishing grounds meant that the states of the EC could move towards the rational exploitation of fishing resources. This, however, depended on being able to find an adequate mechanism for their allocation among member states.

9.4 The development of the CFP

The Treaty of Rome does not specifically mention the development of a CFP, possibly because the industry was small relative to the size of the economies of the Six, and there were more urgent priorities. Also, the industry was subject on the catching side to the influence of other international agencies. However, as trade liberalisation started to affect the less efficient French and Italian fleets, it was clear that help would be required. It took from the mid 1960s to 1970 to agree on a policy. The spur to agreement being the possible accession of new members.

When the original Six launched the CFP in 1970, it was not the ideal organisation to run a fisheries policy, especially on the catching side. One member had no coastline at all, three had only short coastlines and one was a Mediterranean state, and was involved in regulation of fish in the area covered by the CFP.

Not only did EC officials lack experience of the area, but more importantly, the major European fishing nations were not members. To compensate for this, however, the EC had certain advantages. Firstly the EC could win agreement over a broader range of issues than just fishing, so that losses and gains could be traded. Secondly, the EC had some mechanisms to ensure that policies are actually carried through. So despite its imperfections, the EC was superior to organisations like NEAFC. It could of, course, be argued that the best possible solution would be to leave it to nation states once 200-mile limits had been declared, but such a declaration seemed only a distant possibility in 1970.

The regulations adopted in 1970 introduced, first of all, a marketing policy, which involved withdrawing surplus fish in order to support prices, in a method similar to the CAP. Secondly, the principle of non-discriminatory access to Community fishing grounds was introduced. This implied that Community fishing grounds were a shared resource and fishing fleets could operate up to the beaches of member states. Agreement as to the basis of policy came on the very day of the formal application for EC membership of the UK, Denmark, Ireland and Norway. As the four applicants had by far the largest stocks of fish within their 12-mile limits, the move was to generate considerable resentment. Non-discriminatory access took away an important source of protection from foreign boats afforded to inshore fishermen, many of whom lived in communities highly dependent on the industry. The UK, Denmark and Ireland were able to delay full application to the CFP for 10 years as part of the Accession Agreement, but Norway, partly as a result of the proposed CFP, opted to stay out of the EC.

The movement from 12- to 200-mile limits in 1977 increased substantially the EC's role in fisheries management. It had been hoped initially that fishing rights could be renegotiated for the distant-water fleets. There was very little progress in this direction, and so they went into sharp decline. The EC had then to allocate fish largely from its own resources within the communal 200-mile limits. Non-EC fleets were, however, largely excluded from these waters.

The EC's main policy instrument after 1977 was the TAC. This is simply a target level of catches devised on the basis of what fish of each particular type are thought to be available for exploitation within Community waters. The TAC is then broken down and distributed to national fishermen on some agreed basis. It is a highly administered solution of allocation and modified considerably the principle of open access agreed in 1970. The long-term objective of this kind of policy should be a move towards the goal of OSY so that fish stocks would not be depleted, but it was recognised that it would take time to adjust fleet sizes.

Allocation by quotas involves difficult political choices, especially when demand for fish exceeds the supply thought to be available. The EC started with no established basis for policy, consequently the process of decision making was often a very acrimonious one, largely because of what appeared to be incompatible claims to the limited resources. For the UK and Ireland, the ideal solution would have been allocation based on the quantity of fish available within national 200-mile limits. The UK, with its very long coastline and rich fishing grounds, probably had something like 60 per cent of the EC's North Atlantic stock. Traditionally, however, the UK's exploitation of these stocks was not as great as it might have been because of the reliance on its distant-water fleet. This is illustrated in Table 9.2, which also shows the extent to which other members of the EC relied on the wider EC resource.

The initial proposal, put forward by the Commission in 1977, was based on traditional fishing patterns. It offered the UK only 24.4 per cent of the volume of catches. This gave no real compensation for losses of catches off Iceland, and did not reflect the UK's contribution of about 60 per cent of the fish. It became clear at that time that the CFP was even more disadvantageous to the UK than had been first thought. As a consequence it took six years of bitter

Table 9.2 Percentage of catches in other members of the EEC's 200-mile limits – 1973

Netherlands	61
France	46
Belgium	31
West Germany	27
Denmark	18
Ireland	10
Italy	—
UK	—
EEC	20

Source: The Economist, 28 August 1976

dispute to establish the basis of a permanent policy. Three factors helped to bring about the eventual settlement on the 25 January 1983. They were:

1. The recognition that the UK case had some merit.
2. The end of the 10-year postponement of fully open access imposed by the Accession Agreement.
3. The threat posed by the very large Spanish fishing fleet having access to EC waters as a result of membership.

The settlement was actually an agreement of quotas for 1982, the year past. However, it established the basis for future settlements. Table 9.3 sets out one version of the settlement; the EC did not publish its own, thus allowing differing nations to put their own complexion on things.

The quotas given in Table 9.3 apply to what are known as cod equivalents. This is a formula which allows the worth of fish to be standardised as follows: cod (1.0), haddock (1.0), redfish (0.87), whiting (0.86), saithe (0.77), mackerel (0.3). If all fish were taken to be of equal value the UK's quota would be something like 30 per cent.

The agreement was to last 20 years. In addition to the quotas, for a period of 10 years, extra protection was given to some communities particularly dependent on fishing by an exclusive national 6-mile limit, and a larger area where restrictive 12-mile limits applied. Also, in an area off the Shetlands, boat sizes were restricted, and in other areas industrial fishing was prohibited.

Table 9.3 Allocation of quotas for 1982. The basis of future allocation

	Tonnes	%
Belgium	28,900	2.0
Denmark	344,000	24.2
France	183,000	12.9
West Germany	182,000	12.8
Ireland	60,700	4.3
Netherlands	100,800	7.8
UK	509,500	35.8
EEC	1,424,000	99.9

Source: Eurofish Report, 27 January 1983

9.5   Current operation of the CFP

Currently the CFP can be seen to be pursuing six broad sets of objectives. They are:

1. Conserving the supply of fish by the use of quotas and controlling fishing methods.
2. Reducing over-capacity.
3. Avoiding unfair competition in the industry.
4. Preserving employment in the industry.
5. Ensuring orderly marketing.
6. Assimilating the Iberian fleets.

Conservation

Given the finite nature of the resources, conservation will always be the major issue concerning the operation of the CFP. The EC has used quotas and controls over fishing methods to try and balance catches with the supplies available. Generally, it is an area where the policy can be regarded as having some success. In 1985 and 1986 quotas were actually agreed prior to the start of the year, and some stocks, once under pressure, are showing signs of recovery so making more fish available for distribution. Regrettably, this has not been universally true. The 1986 North Sea cod quotas were cut by 18 per cent due to a decline in stocks partly attributed to a combination of biological factors and over-fishing. Immature fish are still being caught in significant quantities, leading to possible pressures on stocks at a later date. In order to combat this, minimum net sizes have been increased, although the degree of compromise which has been required to reach agreement has reduced the impact of these measures. The measures taken in 1986 did not prove to be adequate, as Table 9.4 illustrates, and as a result the gap between allowable catches and actual catches grew significantly. This resulted in savage cuts in quotas for 1987, but it is a measure of the CFP's strength that these were agreed, and will be enforced.

Major problems also exist in the important area of enforcement. There are numerous examples of fishing in excess of quotas, illegal fishing and fraudulent record keeping. The Commission has been slow in taking action against member states, for example infringements which took place in 1980–81 were not dealt with until 1985. Also, the rigour with which member states enforce fishing regulations still varies considerably between member states, with widely varying levels of fines for similar offences.

Table 9.4 Allowable catches and actual catches of North Sea cod and haddock (tonnes)

Year	Cod		Haddock	
	Maximum allowable	Actual	Maximum allowable	Actual
1983	240	237	181	165
1984	215	188	170	133
1985	250	187	207	168
1986	170	147	230	140
1987	125	—	140	—

Source: Commission of the EC. Quoted in *The Independent*, 17 December 1986

As a result of the 1983 settlement, 13 Community fishery inspectors were appointed to supervise the operation of national inspectors. The number was not regarded as being adequate, given the inadequacies of some national inspectorates, and the increased size of the EC's fleet as a result of Spanish and Portuguese membership. As a consequence the Community inspectorate was increased to 22. It has been argued, however, that the only truly efficient method of enforcement would be the establishment of a Community inspectorate that replaced the national officials. Politically, this proposal is unlikely to be acceptable because it threatens national sovereignty.

Reducing capacity

Ideally a fishing fleet should be kept occupied most of its time in order to ensure profitability. If there is over-capacity, and restrictions are placed upon fishing, there is a tendency to under-report catches, and avoid restrictions. Some of the over-capacity in the EC fleet has disappeared, especially in the case of the distant-water vessels of the UK and West Germany. However, spending on restructuring the fleet has not been adequate, despite some ECU 32 million being made available by the EC to be spent supplementing national scrapping schemes. More money, some ECU 44 million, was made available for mothballing boats which simply stores up over-capacity problems for the future.

Avoiding unfair competition

As with most EC policy areas, national governments are involved

131

in some way in promoting the interests of the industry. In the past, there were a multiplicity of national schemes which helped the industry. Some of these, such as fuel subsidies, were not only harmful in that they slowed down the shake-out of excess catching capacity, but they also resulted in excess supplies of fish and depressed prices. The amount and scope of national aid is now restricted in order to avoid this. Money can, however, be spent by national governments improving marketing and developing new fishing grounds, but this is subject to Commission approval.

Preserving employment in the industry

Maintaining fish stocks and regulating the method of their exploitation will have the greatest effect on the number of fishermen the industry can support. The CFP, by giving preference to national fishermen in the band varying between 6 and 12 miles around the coast, is biased towards inshore fishermen and their smaller boats. Added to this, around the Shetland Islands there is a limit to boat sizes. This not only helps to preserve employment in those remote communities dependent on fishing, but it also makes it difficult for larger, more capital-intensive boats to become viable.

Employment in fishing in the EC Nine declined from 154,261 in 1970 to 112,631 in 1981. Curiously, however, the numbers employed in the UK industry actually increased from 21,651 to 23,927 over the same period, despite the demise of the distant-water fleet. This was the result of the expansion of inshore fishing, with labour being substituted for capital. The actual number of full-time fishermen in the UK declined by 1,019 over the period, so the increased numbers were due to an increase in part-time fishermen. The EC has given aid to help those displaced out of the industry, but the extent of this has been limited.

Ensuring orderly marketing

The market support system of the CFP has been in operation since 1970. Since that time it has generated less controversy than the catching side of the policy. The policy is carried out by producer organisations (POs) whose members are the community fishermen (there were about 90 of them in the EC Ten). Membership of the POs is voluntary, and fishermen pay a levy to belong. The Council of Ministers fixes a guide price for different species of fish annually. From this is derived a withdrawal price, and the POs will not sell their members' fish below it. The surplus fish must be disposed of so as not to interfere with normal marketing practices, and must not be used for human consumption. Compensation is paid, but on a sliding scale to discourage catching which will only result in the fish being dumped. Producer organisations are expected to pay a limited amount towards any compensation paid, the rest being made up by EC funds.

Although the system operates on a similar basis to the CAP, the significant difference is that it costs much less, as Table 9.5 indicates.

The cost of the market support is low partly because of the degressive system of compensation. Added to this the EC is a net importer of fish, so that tariffs can be used to discourage cheap imports and maintain prices. Finally, the cost of encouraging exports has been limited, partly because payments are available only on a small range of fish. Also the EC is relatively efficient at processing fish.

Assimilating the Iberian fleets

The accession of Spain and Portugal in January 1986 created the most important challenge currently facing the CFP, for as a consequence the Community has to cope with:

1. A doubling of the number of fishermen;
2. A three-quarter increase in catching capacity;
3. More complex external relations as some member states, especially the Spanish, take a significant portion of their fish outside EC waters.

The Accession Agreement allows for a seven-year period for the industries to adjust to the EC regime, although access to some fishing grounds will not be allowed until at least 1995.

The fishing industries of Spain and Portugal should not be regarded as similar. The Portuguese fleet is old, about 75 per cent being over 15 years old, and only 6,000 of the 16,000 vessels are motorised, the rest being powered by oar and sail. Not unnaturally

Table 9.5 Payments made for market support of the common fisheries policy (ECU million)

Year	1980	1981	1982	1983	1984	1985
Payments	28.0	34.0	25.7	15.6	19.1	23.3

Source: EC Court of Auditors Reports 1986

the fleet mostly confines its activities to the 12-mile coastal limit from where about 80 per cent of the country's catch comes from. A good deal of the rest of the catch is made up of distant-water catches, but most of the fish is sold fresh, because of a lack of freezing and storage capacity. The problem of Portugal's industry is a lack of modernisation and investment.

As a contrast, the average size of the 17,500 vessels that make up the Spanish fleet is very much larger. It contains 2,500 trawlers and 500 freezer ships. The fleet operates in many parts of the world, and has an annual catch of 1.1 million tonnes. This complicates the EC's external fisheries relations as the Commission will have to negotiate with many more non-EC countries to maintain Spanish access. Failure to secure alternative stocks may well result in greater demands for access to the limited Community ones. Within the Community, the major fear is the lack of discipline shown by the Spanish fleet. The Spanish dislike the EC's use of quotas to regulate catches and prefer the use of closed seasons. The fleet has the reputation of frequently ignoring regulations, for example not declaring catches and fishing without licences. Many Spanish fishermen see membership of the EC as a way of unlocking the riches of EC fishing grounds. Countries like the UK, France and Ireland, wish to keep them at bay as long as possible. The Accession Agreement offered little to the Spaniards, but potentially, large numbers of Spanish vessels might re-register in countries like the UK, once free movement of labour becomes fully applicable to the new member states. This could mean that national quotas are circumvented, although member states may still be able to insist that the national quota is landed in the home country.

9.6 Conclusion

Although a number of member states might reflect that they could have done better from the negotiated policy, there seems to be a general acceptance that a reasonable compromise has been achieved. The CFP's success can be measured in two ways. Firstly, its cost is clearly under control, despite providing reasonably secure marketing arrangements. Secondly, the conservation of fish stocks looks reasonably assured, given a willingness to cut quotas when a need arises. Where future problems might emerge is with the assimilation of the Spanish fleet.

Chapter ten
The southern enlargement

In the first 36 years of the Community's existence, the number of member states has doubled. The original Six were fairly homogeneous developed industrial countries, characterised by high levels of economic growth. In retrospect, the integration process proved to be relatively easy, despite often heated arguments, and the existence of areas of economic backwardness, such as southern Italy. The first expansion which took place in 1973 was to the north, and brought membership for the UK, Denmark and Ireland. Although welcomed for their democratic traditions, this was not a comfortable process for the EC. A number of acrimonious disputes, followed before the UK, in particular, was prepared to accept membership as a permanent feature of the political and economic landscape.

The second phase of expansion brought Community membership for three Mediterranean states; Greece in 1981, and Spain and Portugal in 1986. These semi-industrial countries only emerged from a period of dictatorial government in the 1960s. Despite rapid rates of economic growth in the 1970s and early 1970s, they remain relatively poor compared to the rest of the EC. Indeed, as Table 10.1 illustrates, there has been little change in the relative positions of the poorest countries in the league table of incomes per head in the Community since 1960. The gap between the richest and poorest as a percentage of the Community average has narrowed, and overall incomes per head have doubled. The enlargement of the Community has increased the degree of divergence within it, which is an added problem for the policy makers to cope with.

This chapter will survey the economies of the new members and will try and analyse the opportunities and threats that membership poses for them. It will then examine the rationale for expansion from the point of view of the Community and the effects that expansion will have on it. Finally, the implication of the enlargement for non-member Mediterranean states will be discussed.

Table 10.1 Incomes per head compared in the enlarged Community. Real GDP expressed in purchasing power standards

	1960	*1985*
Luxembourg	145.4	129.3
Denmark	126.6	123.9
West Germany	123.4	121.6
France	104.9	114.0
Belgium	103.4	109.8
Netherlands	118.3	106.1
UK	125.8	102.0
Italy	83.5	91.7
Spain	59.9	75.0
Ireland	67.3	70.7
Greece	39.1	57.1
Portugal	32.8	46.2
EC Twelve	100.0	100.0
EC Twelve (1960 100)	100.0	198.2

Source: Commission of the EC *Annual Economic Report* 1986–1987

10.1 The three new members

In 1950, the new members were typical of the southern European economies. They had low incomes per head, were technologically backward and the dominant occupation was agriculture. In the period after 1960 the three economies went through substantial changes, with high rates of economic growth, and a decline in the importance of agriculture. These trends are illustrated in Table 10.2.

The period of transformation of the economies coincided with their greater internationalisation. This consisted of a reduced emphasis on import substitution, and the abandonment of import quotas and tariff reductions, as illustrated in Table 10.3.

The internationalisation of these economies involved a number of other aspects. The level of foreign investment increased, as businesses were attracted by low wage rates, and access to other European markets. There was a degree of technology transfer with the operation of multinational companies in these markets, although not sufficient adequately to modernise much of domestic industry. Tourism started to have its effect, creating jobs in the services

Table 10.2 Employment in main sources of economic activity in 1960 and 1984

	Agriculture		Industry		Service	
	1960[1]	1984[2]	1960[1]	1984[2]	1960[1]	1984[2]
EC Ten	—	7.4	—	34.6	—	58.0
Greece	56	29.4	20	27.8	24	42.7
Portugal	44	23.4	29	34	27	42.2
Spain	42	18	31	32.7	27	49.3

Source: (1) Quoted by A. Williams, 1984; (2) *Basic Statistics of the Community* 23rd edn.

Table 10.3 Tariff protection (annual averages) % value import duties of goods

	Greece	Portugal	Spain
1961–64	86.47	14.40	57.80
1965–69	85.76	10.22	54.66
1970–74	72.02	7.60	48.76
1975–78	56.82	8.70	35.50

Source: Commission of the EC *The EEC and the Mediterranean Basin*

sector and earning valuable foreign exchange. Finally, many workers were attracted to better-paid jobs within the more prosperous European economies. They therefore migrated, but sent home remittances, which helped their home balance accounts.

Each of these economies has its own characteristics despite some of the general features mentioned above, and we shall now look at each one in turn. To begin with Greece, as the first of the three to join the EC, secondly Spain, as the major industrial threat and finally Portugal as the poorest member.

Greece

Greece became the EC's first Associate member as a result of an agreement signed in 1961 and coming into effect in November 1962. This agreement was much more than a simple commercial treaty and stipulated the integration of large parts of the Greek economy, including agriculture, into the EC economy. Even at this early stage, and despite the backwardness of the Greek economy, accession was seen as the ultimate goal. The agreement envisaged the eventual harmonisation of agricultural policies, but its main impact was on manufactures. Here there was to be the removal of tariffs and quotas by 1974, the exception being about 40 per cent of Greek imports of manufactures, which were allowed a 22-year transition period.

The military junta which assumed power in Greece between 1967 and 1974 was deeply unpopular with the Community, and this led to the so-called freezing of relations between the two. In practice, this meant that the existing agreed timetable of events went ahead, so that Greek manufactures enjoyed duty-free access to the Community from 1968, and Greece allowed two-thirds of EC manufactures to enter duty free after 1974. What was delayed, was the process of harmonisation in areas like agriculture. It was during this period of Association that the Greek economy went through a period of dramatic growth well in excess of the world average, OECD average and EC average. Growth rates averaged 7.6 per cent per year in the 1961–70 period and averaged 4.7 per cent in the slower-growing period from 1971 to 1980.

Despite these growth rates, the Greek economy was not in a position to compete on equal terms when it entered the EC in 1981. A great deal of the modernisation that had taken place in the economy was in areas where foreign investment was involved, for example, chemicals, plastics and petroleum. Much of the country's domestic manufacturing remained highly protected by tariff and non-tariff barriers and failed to modernise adequately. The economy's external payments position was balanced by receipts from migrants, and earnings from shipping and tourism.

When Greece joined the Community in 1981, a five-year transition period was agreed in all areas, with the exception of tomatoes and peaches, which would not become part of the CAP until the end of 1987. The Greek economy was not, however, ready for the shock of membership, despite the replacement of tariff barriers with non-tariff barriers. The degree of import penetration increased and growth rates slowed down significantly. In 1981 growth was negative at -0.3 per cent, in 1982 it was -0.2 per cent, and in 1983 it was only 0.3 per cent. Only in 1984 did growth recover to 2.6 per cent, and amidst a growing crisis, it was 2.3 per cent, but in 1986 it was around zero. Greek industry was not able to compete, so that by 1985 it was estimated that 40 per cent of manufacturing was losing money, and industry as a whole was running at a loss. Industrial production was lower in 1985 than in 1979, and the level of investment was lower than in 1972. Trade in agricultural products, which had always been in broad balance with the EC until membership, also drifted into a worrying deficit.

As a result of poor trade performance, a serious payments crisis emerged. In 1980, the balance of payments on the current account showed a surplus of 0.3 per cent of GDP, but by 1985 estimates indicated a deficit of 8.4 per cent of GDP. The result of the poor balance of payments record was that debt accumulated, so that servicing is estimated to take something like 22 per cent of external receipts. Greece did not meet EC requirements for the openness of the economy on the agreed dates. Value added tax had not been introduced, even after many delays, by the end of 1985, and export subsidies and discriminatory taxation were still evident. In response to these external problems, the drachma has been steadily devalued against the ECU in the 1980s. In October 1985 there was a further devaluation, along with the introduction of an import deposit scheme. Importers were expected to place an 80 per cent deposit for luxury goods, and one of 40 per cent for ordinary goods, with the Bank of Greece for a period of six months. The result was a curbing of imports, but at the expense of free trade with the Community. Falling oil prices, and import controls, helped the balance of payments to recover, so that the 1986 deficit on the current account looked like being nearly halved. In order to ride out the crisis, the Community made a loan to the Greeks of ECU 1.75 billion, made in two parts. The first was paid in November 1985, and the second was agreed in December 1986. In return the Greeks were expected to maintain a programme of economic austerity, and phase out their import controls and export subsidies. They also finally introduced VAT in January 1987 as part of the agreement.

The poor performance of the Greek economy cannot be blamed entirely on EC membership. Some of the problems are related to a slowing down in the growth of the world economy. Agricultural productivity increases had slowed down from an average of 2.5 per cent per annum in the 1970s to 1 per cent per annum average in the 1980s. This reflected the structural problems facing the industry, and the poor quality of the land. Domestic politics may also have harmed the prospects of an easy transition period. In 1981 the anti-EC, Panhellenic Socialist Movement (Pasok) was elected. As long as Pasok gave the impression of wanting to remove the country from the EC, industry felt a reduced incentive to adapt. Along with its anti-EC stance, Pasok's policy was to try to right some of the past economic injustices in the country. This was done by running large public sector deficits, and tolerating an inflation rate consistent at around 20 per cent. These domestic policies were generally regarded as one of the main contributions to the economy's external problems.

As Greek membership has continued, the benefits of membership have become more apparent. A combination of tough bargaining and Community generosity has resulted in significant financial benefits for the Greeks. As a result of the CAP, farm incomes rose by 12.7 per cent in the first five years of membership. As Table 10.4 shows, gains from the EC budget have been significant, after a poor start when the Greek bureaucracy was slow to exploit fully available EC funds. To some extent these gains have to be offset against the the cost to the Greek economy of higher prices paid for food imports as a result of the CAP.

Greece has been able to turn to the Community for financial help during its economic crisis and get help on better terms than might have been available elsewhere. Finally, it will gain at least ECU 2 billion from the Integrated Mediterranean Programmes agreed in 1985. This is an ECU 6.6 billion programme over seven years, designed to help the backward Mediterranean areas of existing members. This was regarded by many as a bribe to accept the accession of Spain and Portugal, and certainly reflects the tough stance taken by the Greeks in their national interest.

Such have been the financial gains from membership, that Mr Papandreou, the Greek Prime Minister, told his Parliament in December 1985, that leaving the EC would be 'catastrophic'. This change of heart owed a great deal to the success in pursuing national interests above Community ones. It does, however, indi-

Table 10.4 Gains by Greece from the EC budget 1981/85 (ECU millions)

Year	Contribution to EC own resources	% of EC own	Payments made to Greece	% of all payments
1981	245.5	1.4	394.7	2.4
1982	381.6	1.8	985.9	5.5
1983	377.7	1.6	1,351.4	6.2
1984	355.8	1.4	1,364.0	5.7
1985	388.0	1.5	1,702.8	6.9
Total	1,748.6		5,798.8	

Total cash benefit = ECU 4,050.2

Source: EC Court of Auditors Reports 1986

cate that lessons for the membership of Spain and Portugal can be learned. The shock of membership can easily be underestimated in an attempt to pursue political ideals. Poor countries, with backward industry need cash compensation to meet with the challenge. A lack of generosity can easily lead to disharmony and crisis within the Community.

Spain

Spain is the largest of the three new Mediterranean states to join the EC, and as such presents some of the greatest problems and opportunities for it. With a population in excess of 37 million, a more developed industrial structure and higher incomes per head than either Greece or Portugal, it is likely that Spanish accession will have a significant impact on the Community.

The Industrial Revolution came late to Spain, and yet it was to become one of the miracle economies of Europe in the 1960s. In 1950 it was backward, with living standards actually lower than in 1930. The reasons for this retardation were the effects of the 1930s recession, the bitter Civil War and the policy of autarky pursued by the dictator, General Franco. The policy of autarky involved an overvaluation of the currency, trade restrictions and the promotion of import substitution. This policy was only partly as a result of deliberate choice. In the period 1946–50, Spain was isolated by United Nations sanctions, which were lifted as a consequence of the cold war.

In the 1950s the economy grew by a rate in excess of 5 per cent annually, although, of course, from a low base. In this period of growth there was a high degree of state of direction, although the effectiveness of this has been the subject of debate. By 1959 pressures from the balance of payments forced the introduction of the Stabilisation Plan. This involved a regularisation of the exchange rate, a sharp devaluation, some liberalisation of trade and a relaxation of price controls. From this time onward the growth rates of the economy accelerated to an average of 6.9 per cent per annum in the period 1959–73.

The reasons for the rapid growth of the Spanish economy are similar to those of Greece, with the movement from the land into manufacturing and the service sectors being particularly important. The introduction of new technology was also important, and here the foreign-based multinationals played a particularly important role, especially in areas like motor vehicle production. Domestically, the activities of the state holding company, Institutor

Nacional de Industria (INI) was responsible for investing in a number of key sectors. Added to this, capital formation increased because of high profits due to a highly regressive taxation system and artificially low wages. Under the Franco regime, normal trade-union activity was not permitted. Typically, the Spanish economy suffered trade deficits throughout the period of rapid growth, but these were balanced by capital imports, receipts from migrants and tourism.

There is doubt that the rapid growth of the 1960s, owed something to the contact with the rapidly growing economies of Western Europe. However, the Spanish economy was not particularly open to foreign trade. Unlike Portugal, Spain did not belong to EFTA, nor did she have an Association agreement with the EC as Greece had. In fact, it was not until 1970 that Spain signed a trade agreement with the Community. In retrospect this protectionism might well be regarded as a mistake, for growth rates may well have been as high if the economy had been more open. An open economy would have encouraged domestic enterprises to cope with international competition, instead of hiding behind trade barriers, which simply stored up adjustment problems for later.

After the 1973–74 oil shock, Spain's economy slowed down with real growth only averaging 1.5 per cent a year between 1974 and 1982, which was below the EC average of 1.8 per cent. Growth rates in Spain fell below 1 per cent after the second oil shock of 1979, but recovered to an average of 2.4 per cent per year in the four years to the end of 1986, which was above the Community average.

Part of the problem was simply connected to the dependence of the economy on cheap oil. Indeed, about 70 per cent of Spain's energy is imported. The slowing of growth elsewhere meant that Spanish migrants were no longer as welcome as in the past. Because tourism did not grow at the same rate as in the past, this had an effect on the important construction sector. At the same time, pressures were increasing from the NICS who were expanding in similar areas to the Spanish, for example in steel, textiles and shoes. Finally, on the domestic front, adjustment to the oil shock of 1973–74 was slow. Also, with the death of Franco, workers were no longer prepared to accept the wage restrictions of the past. These factors gave rise to a potentially severe bout of inflation, and a pattern of rising unemployment which reached about 20 per cent at the time of Spanish membership of the Community.

Spain first applied for an Association agreement with the EC as early as 1962, but this was not acceptable to the Community on political grounds, as it would appear to legitimise the Franco regime. In 1970 a trade agreement was signed, which was something less than Spain had hoped for. The agreement offered little in the way of concessions in the agricultural sector; indeed, when the UK joined the EC in 1973, this sector found itself facing greater discrimination. In industrial goods there was a reciprocal reduction in tariffs. This was particularly beneficial to Spain as it had far higher tariffs in the first place, plus a whole range of non-tariff barriers. It led to a situation where exports to the Community carried minimal tariffs, but for products like cars it was almost impossible to penetrate the Spanish market, because of a tariff of nearly 40 per cent.

The impact of EC membership on Spain

The balance of benefits to Spain from EC membership are likely to be political in the early years of entry. The experience of Greece indicates that economic benefits can be elusive in the early years, because of the speed at which import penetration takes place and the difficulty of adjusting domestic production.

A seven-year timetable for the removal of tariffs was agreed between Spain and the EC. The lowering of tariffs is more likely to help those who wish to sell into Spanish markets than exporters from Spain. This is because tariffs are already low into the EC so gains in this direction are likely to small. Producers for the domestic Spanish economy have largely been well sheltered by non-tariff barriers and tariff barriers. This has, in the past, reduced the incentive to modernise these parts of industry. The degree of protection will fall from a much higher level, and so adjustment will have to be fairly rapid. To help this process the Spanish Government has made attempts to encourage modernisation of domestic industry in recent years. An example of this being the 1983 Reconversion and Reindustrialisation Law, which covers areas which are already sensitive in the EC context, such as steel, ship-building, textiles and home appliances.

Some multinational producers are expected to do well although they will not enjoy the exclusive, tariff-free access to the Spanish market any longer. They, along with other Spanish exporters, lost export subsidies because of the introduction of VAT on 1 January 1986. Prior to the introduction of VAT, producers were able to claim back more tax than they paid when they exported goods. Large companies had already adjusted to international competition, and were able to exploit the cheaper Spanish labour. Since membership, more international companies have shown an interest in a

Spanish location. The future of these companies established in Spain will ultimately depend on the extent to which protectionist tendencies continue within the world economy. If protectionism increases, Spain's ample supply of cheap labour may attract even more producers, although this is by no means certain, given that Portuguese wage costs are even lower. If, however, world markets remain relatively open, the Spanish economy may face intense competition from the NICs in many of its traditional areas, because they too have a comparative advantage with cheap labour.

Despite the fact that about 15 per cent of the population work on the land, Spain normally has a slight overall trade deficit in agricultural products, although in the past it has had a slight surplus with the EC. As a result of membership, there has been some trade diversion from cheaper non-EC suppliers for items like beef and cereals, and this has particularly upset their American suppliers. Also, Spanish dairy farmers have faced severe competition from the more efficient EC producers. Despite the fact that the CAP favours northern European producers, Spain is still likely to benefit in the Mediterranean products, where she enjoys a comparative advantage. Spanish produce will displace not only the products of other EC growers, but also those from North Africa who have privileged access to the market. The areas where they are likely to do well are salads, fresh vegetables and citrus fruit. In the case of wine, Spanish production is a considerable embarrassment to the Community, and the cost of support to the CAP has been controlled by offering guaranteed prices for only 27.5 million hectolitres of table wine. Agriculture should also gain from special grants for groups like hill farmers.

Early indications are that in the first nine months of membership, Spain's deficit in agricultural products increased from $7 million to $237 million compared to the year before. Overall exports to the Community rose by 6 per cent in the first nine months of membership, while imports rose by 25 per cent. Total imports from the Community rose from 35 per cent of all imports to 48 per cent while exports rose from 50 per cent to 61 per cent. Spain's traditional trade surplus with the Community disappeared in the first few months of membership, but this did not cause balance of payment problems, because Spain benefited substantially as a result of falling oil prices. The surge of imports could, however, become a problem if oil prices were to rise again. There is a temptation to see the economic issues entirely in terms of the trade balance, but it should be remembered that the level of unemployment in Spain exceeds 20 per cent on a persistent basis.

If the effect of import penetration is that this figure does not fall, then there is a possibility of reaction against the Community on this issue.

Finally, the CFP is of great importance to Spain as a major consumer and catcher of fish. However, this was discussed in Chapter 9.

Portugal

Portugal is the poorest member of the EC despite rapid economic growth in the period from the 1950s until the general slow-down as a result of the first oil shock. The lack of development in the past can partly be traced back to the authoritarian regimes of Antonio Salazar (1932–68) and Mancello Caetano (1968–74), who regarded industrialisation as being relatively unimportant, and concentrated much of their efforts in the later period on a disastrous colonial war. Portugal did not suffer the kind of political and economic isolation imposed upon the Spanish after the Second World War. However, the futile efforts to hold on to colonies in the 1960s and early 1970s were very much against the tide of opinion in Western Europe, and did cause strains in political relations.

Throughout the period of dictatorial conservatism, much of the country's large-scale industry and banking was controlled by a small number of families. It was estimated that 300 of the 411 most important companies in the country were controlled by only seven private groups. In the earlier periods especially, foreign direct investment was discouraged. Many small- and medium-sized domestic enterprises were, however, inefficient and starved of capital. Such was the contrast between opportunities within the country, and those elsewhere, that large numbers emigrated causing actual population declines. It was estimated by the OECD[1] that in 1983 40.4 per cent of Portugal's population actually lived abroad, with 12.3 per cent residing in Europe and 28.1 per cent in the rest of the world. This contrasts with Spain, where some 5.6 per cent reside abroad. What it did do for the Portuguese economy was to ensure that there was a steady stream of migrants' remittances coming back into the country which took care of much of the balance of payments pressures associated with growth and the attempts to maintain the Empire.

In the 1951–60 period, Portugal achieved an average growth rate of 4.4 per cent, this increased to 6.4 per cent in the 1960s. Along with this came a period of rapid change, with large numbers leaving the land. Because of its political standing, Portugal was not able to join the EC, but as a result of signing the Stockholm Convention in 1960, she joined EFTA. This was probably not due to any great European commitment, but an attempt to maintain access to UK markets. The terms of entry gave Portugal a much longer period to adjust to free trade than the other members, but did provide a spur for those sectors of the economy affected by trade to improve their efficiency. Over the period 1960–72, exports to Western Europe increased from 44.5 per cent of the total to 64.4 per cent, moving the country firmly within the European ambit. From 1972, Portugal's position with regard to the UK and Denmark came under threat because of their membership of the EC. This was resolved by the free trade area agreement signed in 1972, which allowed for the elimination of tariffs on Portuguese goods into the Community by 1977, the exception being with clothing, textiles and cork manufactures which were not to be allowed free access until 1983. Free access to Portuguese markets was not to occur until 1985. In practice, the agreement was not as generous as those between the EC and Spain and Greece, as there were important restrictions on areas where the Portuguese might have expected to do well. Also, access for imports into Portugal were less subject to non-tariff barriers which Greece and Spain employed so readily. Despite the relative poorness of the agreement, exports from Portugal to Western Europe increased to 72.9 per cent of total exports by 1982.

The collapse of the Caetano regime came in 1974, as a result of the burdens of the colonial wars, and the effects of the first oil shock. The transition to a capitalist democracy was not, however, a smooth one, despite the bloodless nature of the revolution. Major sectors of the economy were nationalised, largely for political reasons; an estimated 700,000 people returned from the former colonies, about half of which were of working age; and agriculture drifted into decline. Unemployment trends towards the end of the 1970s were inevitably upward, although they are difficult to judge in the context of an economy like that of Portugal. This is because of the widespread underemployment in sectors like agriculture, and government insistence that companies retain labour despite it being surplus to requirements.

In order to help Portugal through its transition to democracy, the EC gave financial help in the form of loans with subsidised rates of interest, and improved access to Community markets for Portuguese products. On their part, the Portuguese were permitted to increase certain tariffs to protect their markets. In the period of the late 1970s, growth was at a respectable 4 per cent, although it did slow down, along with the rest of the world economy, in the early 1980s. In order to overcome the problem of a severe payments deficit, the decreasing value of the currency and an inflation rate consistently in excess of 20 per cent, the Socialist Government launched an austerity programme just prior to accession. This meant that there was a decline in real incomes, and home demand was squeezed, forcing a substantial increase in exports. It had the desired effect, however, in that the deficit on balance of payments was removed and the inflation rate started to abate. Growth was resumed in the economy in 1985 and 1986.

The impact of EC membership on Portugal

As with the other new members, the benefits of membership are uncertain. Like Spain, the transition period for industrial goods will be 7 years, while it will be 10 years for agricultural produce. Value added tax will be phased in over the first three years of membership, but there should not be the kind of adaptation problems that have faced the Greeks and Spanish because their economy has been used to a lower level of protection in recent years. Portuguese industry should be competitive in the labour-intensive sectors like textiles and footwear, simply because wages are almost at Third World levels. If we compare earnings, we find that in 1985 Portuguese textile workers earned $1.28 per hour compared with $3.87 in Spain and $7.54 in West Germany.[2] The fact that Portugal is now a member of the EC should mean that the position of these industries is reasonably assured, in that they cannot be discriminated against. However, this does not mean that these industries are without their structural problems, and they still need to modernise.

Almost inevitably the first effect of membership that started to manifest itself was a return to the problems with the balance of payments. As with Spain, lower oil prices were a benefit, but by the early part of 1987 it was clear that the gap in balance of payments with the Community had worsened the country's overall trade position. In the first year of membership, imports from the EC had grown by 35.5 per cent, while exports to the Community had grown by only 16.1 per cent. The area where Portugal's economy is at its weakest is agriculture. As Table 10.5 shows, the industry has actually been in decline in recent years.

A combination of fragmentation of holdings, political disturbances and extremely harsh production conditions means that the country imports something like 60 per cent of its food. This is

Table 10.5 Comparative yields for main agricultural products

Total EEC and selected southern European countries	Portugal		Greece		Spain		EEC	
	1970–73	1979–80	1970–73	1979–80	1970–73	1979–80	1970–73	1979–80
Wheat	35.5	23.0	55.6	60.5	35.9	41.8	100	100
Rye	22.2	17.2	39.1	45.1	28.9	31.9	100	100
Barley	20.2	15.2	58.1	59.9	46.5	51.6	100	100
Oats	17.5	14.0	43.8	42.4	30.8	35.8	100	100
Maize	26.5	21.9	65.9	108.9	72.7	84.9	100	100
Rice	88.4	77.4	103.4	87.9	128.6	112.3	100	100
Potatoes	40.5	34.5	51.5	55.3	51.8	57.4	100	100

Source: OECD 1984 *Report on Portugal*, p 20

despite the fact that 23.8 per cent of the working population are employed in agriculture. Very low productivity and chronic under-employment means that it contributes only about 9 per cent of GDP. Prices of key products like wheat and milk are actually higher in Portugal than in the EC, so the transition period will have to be used to reduce prices to the EC level. At the same time, an ECU 700 million aid programme has been launched to try and modernise the sector. Although wheat prices are, for example, some 50 per cent cheaper in the EC, it is still the case that trade diversion will take place. This is because world prices are cheaper still. If the Portuguese agricultural sector does not improve its performance, membership will add greatly to the country's import bill.

What is clear about the Portuguese case is that the country is so poor that a very great effort will be needed to make membership work. In particular, it looks likely that special programmes will need to be launched just for this one economy. The main effort will have to be in the agricultural areas, if for no other reason than that food imports may mean that Portugal will be a net contributor to the EC budget without specific help there. Aid will also be required to modernise industry and social infrastructure. Finally, it should be noted that the fishing fleet is also very primitive, but this situation is discussed in Chapter 9.

10.2 Qualification of membership

According to Article 237 of the Treaty of Rome, any European state may apply to become a member of the EC. There is no specific requirement that the state be democratic. However, because the Treaty includes provision for free movement of people, services and capital, and the fact that there is a competition policy means that member states are likely to be market economies to a significant extent. Also, the existence of direct elections to the European Parliament, provided for under Article 138, leaves room for little else but democracies. Added to this, on 5 April 1977, the Presidents of the European Parliament, the Commission and the Council of Ministers, made a joint declaration stressing the importance of protecting human rights so that it is unlikely that any country not respecting democracy and human rights would have a place in the EC.

10.3 The rationale for enlargement

An ideal partner should have something like the following characteristics:

1. Be so rich that it does not require financial help and actually contribute towards the Community's resources;
2. Have no industrial sector facing a crisis;
3. Not be a surplus producer of agricultural products;
4. Have no regions of the economy which are substantially backward;
5. Have a population which supports the European ideal and the liberal democratic tradition.

The three new members do not, of course, match up to the above specifications at all well; indeed there are no ideal applicants. However, enlargement is a sign of the organisation's fundamental vitality, and there are specific political and economic reasons for the expansion. The political reasons are:

1. It will help to preserve liberal democracy within these formerly totalitarian states.
2. It will help to strengthen European unity.
3. The Mediterranean region is one of the most complex and politically unstable regions of world politics. The addition of the three new members should be a contribution towards stability, and ensure the place of these countries within the Western Alliance.
4. It will enhance the Communities' standing in world diplomacy.

The economic reasons are probably of more direct consequence to the operation of the Community. They are:

1. It will increase the size of the Community market, which should increase the trading opportunities available.
2. Material advantage should accrue to the new applicants, not only from trade but also from transfers via the Community's policies.
3. The increase in the size of the Community will consolidate the EC's position as the world's foremost trading block and as a consequence its weight in international trade negotiations.
4. The accession of Spain and Portugal in particular provides important trade links with South America and Africa.

10.4 The effects of increased membership on the operation of the Community

Enlargement of the Community in 1986 involved an increase in the size of the Commission from 14 to 17, the Council of Ministers from 10 to 12, the European Parliament from 434 to 518, the ESC from 156 to 189 and the ECJ from 11 to 13. Added to this, two new languages were added to the Community list, and about 1,500 new eurocrats arrived in Brussels, displacing a number of established personnel.

Until Greek membership in 1981, only one out of the Nine members could be described as relatively poor. Now four out of the Twelve are in this category. This greater divergence within the Community will, to a certain extent, polarise the interests of member states between rich and poor, North and South. It will inevitably effect the operation of institutions and the decision-making process. The most immediate impact on the Parliament in 1986 was that the political balance shifted to the left as a result of being joined by the nominees from the Portuguese and Spanish Parliaments. In the case of the Council of Ministers, the likelihood is that it will become ever more difficult to reconcile the national differences that constantly slow down the development of the Communities in spite of the Single European Act. What appears to have developed is a 'tomato pact', with the Mediterranean countries being joined by Ireland in pushing for more spending on social policy and regional policy, and making that the price of agreement to other changes. Pessimists believe that there is a possibility that the Community may develop in different directions, with either a two-tier or multi-tier Community emerging, with either regional or broad policy coalitions being formed. If there is a failure to reach agreement about issues of importance, this may be resolved by some members going forward on their own with different stages of integration emerging.

The new members accepted the *acquis communautaire* as part of their price of membership. That is, they must abide by the body of law and policy already established. Although the new members participated in the decision-making process from the start, both new and existing members required time to adjust to the new situation. It will take until the end of 1995 before the new members are fully integrated in all respects.

Spain and Portugal will need time to adjust their economies to that absence of tariffs against Community goods in general, while the EC Ten feel particularly threatened in specific areas like textile production. It will take seven years to integrate industry fully; however, the very complex nature of agriculture means that this sector will not become integrated for 10 years. As Table 10.5 showed, productivity levels in the agricultural sector are well below that of the Community in the area of northern farm products, so that it will take time for the new members to adjust to competition for products like milk. Among the EC Ten, the threat is specifically that posed by Spanish producers of Mediterranean products – not only will northern hot-house producers face intense competition, but also the other Mediterranean states in the EC, that is, France Italy and Greece. In order to allow these countries to adapt to this new competition, the Community has set aside ECU 6.6. billion for modernisation of these regions. This money is part of what is described as the Integrated Mediterranean Programme.

As Table 10.6 shows, the new members all have considerable numbers of their nationals working in the Community.

Given the long-term nature of the current recession and the problem of chronic unemployment throughout the Community, it is hardly surprising that restrictions were placed on free movement of workers as part of the transition arrangements. Spanish and Portuguese workers already established in the EC Ten countries will have full rights immediately. New immigrants will enjoy full rights of establishment until 1993 with the exception of those seeking work in Luxembourg. Because a third of all workers in Luxembourg are foreigners already, they have been given the right to deny free entry until 1996.

10.5 The financial costs of two new members

This is an area of considerable uncertainty, largely because it is not clear how trade patterns will develop. One area where a high degree of trade diversion is likely is agricultural products into Portugal. This payment of higher prices for food will clearly impose a

Table 10.6 Migrant workers from the new members in the EC Nine in 1979

Greece	166,000
Portugal	476,000
Spain	349,000

Source: Commission of EC *The EEC and the Mediterranean Basin*

considerable burden on the Portuguese, and there is a very good case for directly compensating for this. In other areas of trade, moving away from non-EC supplies in order to avoid the payment into the EC's budget via the CCT is desirable.

In order to reduce the financial burden for the new members there is a mechanism for budgetary compensation in the Treaty of Accession, which provides for VAT refunds on the following scale:

Table 10.7

Year	%
1986	87
1987	70
1988	55
1989	40
1990	25
1991	5

The reducing scale of VAT refunds is designed to avoid the new members being net contributors to the EC budget by promoting an expenditure-side solution. This is based upon ever-increasing use of Community funds such as the ERDF and the ESF. To capitalise on the opportunities offered by these funds, the new members need to gain experience of them quickly, in order to generate the kind of schemes that qualify. In the case of ERDF, this may be difficult because of the time element. Typically, about 70 per cent of ERDF money goes on infrastructure schemes which can take a number of years to design. Also, in the past no more than 50 per cent of Community funds has been available towards the cost of schemes so that other sources of finance are required. This may be difficult to arrange, especially in very poor areas.

Although the money is available, these relatively poor countries may not be able to take full advantage of it. The same qualification applies to loans made available via EC institutions like the EIB and the ECSC. For borrowing to be a success there must be adequate resources to stand the pace of repayments. This means that perhaps the poverty of some regions of Spain and the whole of Portugal may be such that other solutions have to be found. The ESF does offer some hope, and in the first year of membership the Iberian members managed to generate sufficient schemes to take around a quarter of the total fund. If the expenditure-side solution should fail, however, and a financial crisis emerges, then it may lead to a further budget crisis.

10.6 The effects on trade relations with non-member states

The expansion of the EC has implications for trade relations with non-member states. In areas like agriculture, a degree of trade diversion is inevitable. The supplies of products like wheat and beef to Spain and Portugal from outside the EC have been dislodged in favour of the higher-priced CAP supplies. On the other hand, some trade creation will take place, particularly as the highly protected Spanish market becomes subject to lower EC tariffs for industrial goods, and therefore more easily accessible to non-EC producers (an issue discussed in Ch. 3).

The exporters to the EC will face increased competition within the Community as a result of the addition of new members with relatively low labour costs. Prior to the expansion, the Lomé countries and many Mediterranean states enjoyed superior access to Community markets, particularly in relation to Spain. As the transition period comes to an end, these countries will find that the value of their privileged access is diluted. Less developed countries will find their exports under greatest pressure where both they and the new members are strongest, notably textiles and Mediterranean agricultural products. Despite short-term provisions adopted to maintain their positions, the likelihood is that these non-member countries will find that the EC market is less certain, especially if the crisis in these sensitive sectors worsens.

10.7 Conclusion

The outcome of this most recent enlargement is difficult to predict. In the early stages of expansion negotiations, there was a great deal of talk of the political benefits to be gained. As negotiations continued, it became apparent that the problems arising from the economic divergence within the Community might be considerable. The Greek experience has shown us that economies do not easily adjust to membership. If they do not, the likelihood is there will be increasing demands for financial compensation. Given the fragile state of the Community budget, these may be difficult to meet. Dissatisfaction over financial matters can easily spill over into the political and decision-making process of the Community, and so cause ever greater paralysis. There is also a danger of a splitting off of countries within the Community with a separation in terms of their preparedness to move forward with the integration process.

This gloomy view of the expansion is, of course, largely the result of uncertainty about the future. The fact that Greek membership no longer seems in doubt, and that democracy in that country now seems better established, may after all indicate that the political advantages may be considerable. Also, if the world recession ends and growth rates improve, then some of the resource implications may not be so severe.

To many, the current enlargement to the south is as far as the Community should go in terms of absorbing the poorer states of Europe. Any application from the Scandinavian states would be regarded favourably, but the prospect of the membership of Turkey is greeted with dismay, especially by the Greeks who see the Turks as traditional enemies. In 1987 the unthinkable came one stage closer with the application by Turkey for membership. The very poor record of Turkey in terms of human rights, the fragile state of its democracy and the weakness of its economy seem to rule out early membership. In the future, however, the lessons learnt from Spanish and Portuguese membership might have to be put to use in order to make a Community of Thirteen work.

10.8   References

1. OECD *Outlook* 1985.
2. *Financial Times* 15 November 1985.

Part two

Chapter eleven
Examination questions

Examination questions in EC studies generally require candidates to consider the wider political, economic, social and legal issues of the problem set. Where a question concerns one discipline area, the emphasis should be on that area, but candidates should refer to constraints imposed by other factors. Most question papers require four or five answers in three hours, and they seek to test one or more of the following:

1. The candidate's ability to explain and apply the theoretical concepts that underpin the issue being discussed.
2. The rationale of the policy area being examined.
3. The current status of the policy and the problems associated with implementing it.

Before answering a question, it is important to set out a brief plan. This should contain all the points to be included in the answer presented in a logical order. A detailed plan for two possible questions follows.

Q1 *Examine the case for the European Community adopting an aggressive export strategy in order to rid itself of surplus agricultural production.*

(i) The central role of the CAP within the Community should be stressed.

(ii) Analyse the problem surplus production poses for the Community. In particular the burden it places upon the budget should be examined.

(iii) Outline the difficulties of disposing of surpluses by cutting back on production within the Community. Mention should be made of the use of quotas, price cuts and set-aside schemes.

(iv) The benefits of an aggressive export strategy should now be analysed, including the benefits it would have for farmers, in that they would not have to restrict production to the extent that they might have with other policies. The benefits for political cohesion should be mentioned.

(v) The arguments against should include not only the cost aspects of dumping of surplus production, but the implications that the policy would have on international trade relations. It is likely that other producers of food in the world would object strongly as prices inevitably fall. This might do damage not only to agricultural trade, but if a trade war developed, this might damage other areas of trade.

Q2 *Under what circumstances is a country likely to gain from membership of a common market?*

(i) The distinction between a common market and a customs union should be examined, and their likely contributions towards economic and political integration should be outlined.

(ii) The static trade effects of customs union membership should be explained, in particular the benefits of trade creation and the problem of trade diversion should be stressed.

(iii) The implications of the dynamic effects of trade should then be discussed, with reference to the likely benefits to be gained from economies of scale.

(iv) Explain more fully the implications of non-tariff barriers, and the effect that free movement of people, capital and the harmonisation of business law is likely to have on the member economies.

(v) Remember to make the point that the gains from membership are not likely to be automatic. There are always going to be some states which will gain more than others.

In order to be well prepared for an inter-disciplinary examination in European studies, it is important to practise the kind of answers you will write. A first step would be to attempt to answer the two questions shown above, using the detailed plans provided, within a time limit of 45 minutes. Remember to try and stick to the main point of the question and not to be side-tracked.

Now tackle the following questions using the hints provided.

Q3 *Analyse the likely effects that increased membership will have on the operations of the European Community.*

Hints

- Remember that this question largely concerns the operation of the Community's institutions and policies. Do not spend too long analysing each policy area, but try to look at the main themes.
- The new members in the 1980s were poor semi-industrial countries, and have different interests and needs from many of the existing members.
- The most important considerations are therefore the extent to which they will affect the decision-making process, their demands on the budget and the implications for the CAP.
- Do not forget that many of the potential issues of conflict arose when the Community expanded in 1973.

Q4 *Assess the effectiveness of quotas as a method of controlling the excess production within the European Community.*

Hints

- Quotas are used as a policy instrument to control excess production in agriculture, fishing, steel and road transport. It would be best to restrict observations to just one or two of these sectors.
- Outline the kind of policy problem they are designed to deal with, and the difficulties of using market-based solutions to solve them.
- Set out the long-term as well as short-term problems of using quotas, not forgetting the political difficulties of winning a realistic agreement.

Q5 *'The European Monetary System can reasonably be regarded as a first step towards European Monetary Union'* Discuss.

Hints

- Make it clear that any movement towards EMU requires a considerable degree of integration in a number of policy areas which it is difficult to foresee at the present time. Some discussion of the problems of maintaining a fixed rate of exchange is important.
- The EMS was always seen as a very limited device designed to promote a degree of monetary stability within the EC. Outline the limited success of the EMS.

Q6 *Consider the case for a Community approach towards promoting new technology as against one centred on the member states.*

Hints

- This is typical of many questions which analyse the benefits of collective as against individual action to solve problems. Remember to analyse each in turn.
- Despite any enthusiasm for a complete Community-based policy, remember that the amount of resources involved would be considerable, and therefore there are implications for the EC budget.
- Do not forget that this kind of extension of industrial policy has a political purpose as well as an economic one.

Appendix one

The Single European Act

The Luxembourg European Council held on the 2–3 December 1985, agreed to changes in the treaties and institutions of the EC. These were as follows.

1. The scope of the treaties was to be enlarged

This meant that six new policy objectives were added to the Treaty of Rome:

1. The completion of the internal market of the EC by 1992.
2. Member states should cooperate in economic and monetary policy. The European Monetary System is included in the Treaty for the first time, although its inclusion is mainly of symbolic importance.
3. Harmonisation and improvement in the working environment.
4. Strengthening economic and social cohesion by giving particular emphasis to reducing backwardness in least-favoured regions.
5. The scientific and technological basis of industry to be improved by carrying out research, technological development and demonstration programmes.
6. The quality of the environment to be protected and improved.

2. Decision making was to be made more efficient

The system of qualified majority voting was extended mostly in the area of the new policy objectives. This is likely to be of major importance in the attempt to complete the internal market by 1992. Some sensitive areas are excluded, for example directives with regard to training and access to professions, the harmonisation of indirect taxation and matters relating to the free movement of people. Action on the environmental programme will also require an unanimous vote.

3. The role of the European Parliament was to be enhanced

For the first time the word 'Parliament' replaces the word 'Assembly' in the treaties. The changes mean that Parliament can pronounce on the final decisions of the Council of Ministers. This procedure only has effect where the Council acts by qualified majority voting.

4. European cooperation in foreign policy was to be codified

This is an area not covered by the existing treaties. It calls for members to endeavour to formulate and implement a European foreign policy.

The Single European Act required the agreement of the parliaments of the member states, and so its implementation was not expected until late 1987 or early 1988. One of the most contentious issues for member parliaments was the extent to which it eroded the rights of national governments. Also, the provision for political cooperation appeared to conflict with Irish neutrality.

Appendix two

Useful addresses

Commission of the European Communities,
Rue de la Loi 200,
1049 Brussels   Tel: 235 1111

Council of the European Communities,
Rue de la Loi 170,
1048 Brussels   Tel: 234 6111

European Parliament,
General Secretariat,
Centre Européen,
Plateau du Kirchberg,
2929 Luxembourg   Tel: 43001

Economic and Social Committee,
Rue Ravenstein 2,
1000 Brussels   Tel: 512 3920

Court of Justice,
Plateau du Kirchberg,
2925 Luxembourg   Tel: 43031

Court of Auditors,
29 rue Alderingen,
1118 Luxembourg   Tel: 47731

European Investment Bank,
100 boulevard Konrad Adenauer,
2950 Luxembourg   Tel: 43791

Committee of Permanent
Representatives,
UK Representation (UKREP),
6 Rond Point Schuman,
1040 Brussels   Tel: 230 6205

In the UK

Commission of the European Communities,
London Office,
8 Storey's Gate,
London SW1P 3AT   Tel: 01–222 8122

There are also European Commission offices at:

Edinburgh	Tel: 031–225 2058
Cardiff	Tel: 0222 371631
Belfast	Tel: 0232 240708

European Parliament,
London Information Office,
2 Queen Anne's Gate,
London SW1H 9BU   Tel: 01–222 0411

European Investment Bank,
UK Liaison Office,
23 Queen Anne's Gate,
London SW1H 9BU   Tel: 01–222 2933

Appendix three

Lomé III Convention countries

Angola
Antigua & Barbuda
Bahamas
Barbados
Belize
Benin
Botswana
Burkina Faso
Burundi
Cameroon
Cape Verde
Central African
   Republic
Chad
Comoros
Congo
Djibouti
Dominica
Equatorial Guinea
Ethiopia
Fiji
Gabon
Gambia

Ghana
Grenada
Guinea
Guinea-Bissau
Guyana
Ivory Coast
Jamaica
Kenya
Kiribati
Lesotho
Liberia
Madagascar
Malawi
Mali
Mauritania
Mauritius
Mozambique
Niger
Nigeria
Papua New Guinea
Rwanda
St Christopher &
   Nevis

St Lucia
St Vincent &
   Grenadines
São Tomé & Principe
Senegal
Seychelles
Sierra Leone
Solomon Islands
Somalia
Sudan
Suriname
Swaziland
Tanzania
Togo
Tonga
Trinidad & Tobago
Tuvalu
Uganda
Vanuatu
Western Samoa
Zaire
Zambia
Zimbabwe

Selected bibliography

Chapter two

Denton G 1984 Re-structuring the EC budget: implications of the Fontainebleau Agreement *Journal of Common Market Studies* XXIII (2) 117–40

Holland S 1980 *Uncommon Market*. Macmillan

House of Lords 1985 2nd Report – Select Committee on the European Communities, Session 1984–85. *Fontainebleau and After: Decisions on Future Financing for the Community*, 29 Jan. 1985 (66). HMSO

House of Lords 1985 14th Report – Select Committee on the European Communities, Session 1984–85 *European Union*, 23 July 1985 HL6. HMSO

Lodge J (ed.) 1983 *Institutions and Policies of the European Community*. Francis Pinter

Wallace H 1980 *Budgetary Politics: The Finances of the European Communities*. George Allen and Unwin

Wallace H, Wallace W and Webb C 1983 *Policy Making in the European Community* (2nd edn). John Wiley

Chapter three

Commission of the EC 1985 *Completing the Internal Market*. Office for Official Publications of the EC, Luxembourg

Cosgrove-Twitchett C 1981 *Harmonisation Between Britain and the European Community*. Macmillan

Hine R C 1985 *The Political Economy of European Trade*. Wheatsheaf Books

House of Lords 1982 17th Report – Select Committee on the

European Communities, Session 1981–82. *The Internal Market*, HL 204. HMSO

Owen N 1983 *Economies of Scale Competitiveness and Trade Patterns Within the European Community*. Oxford University Press

Swann D 1984 *The Economics of the Common Market*. Pelican

Vaulont Nikolaus 1980 *The Customs Union of the European Economic Community* Office for Official Publications of the EC, Luxembourg

Chapter four

Hine R C 1985 *The Political Economy of European Trade*. Wheatsheaf Books

Lodge J (ed.) 1983 *Institutions and Policies of the European Community*. Francis Pinter

Smith M 1983 *Trade Relations Between the European Community and the United States: Common Course on Divergent Paths*? University Association for Contemporary European Studies

Spero D E 1985 *The Politics of International Economic Relations* (3rd edn). George Allen and Unwin

Stevens C 1984 *EEC and the Third World: A Survey. No. 4 Renegotiating Loans*. Hodder and Stoughton

Chapter five

Coffey P 1984 *The European Monetary System: Past, Present and Future*. Martinus Nijhoff

House of Commons 1985 19th Report from the Treasury and Civil Service Committee, Session 1984–5 *The European Monetary System*. Vol I *Report*; Vol II *Minutes of Evidence*, 20 Oct. 1985 57-v. HMSO

House of Commons 1985 Treasury and Civil Service Committee, Session 1984–85 *Memoranda on the European Monetary System* 24 July 1985 57 111. HMSO

House of Lords 1983 5th Report – Select Committee on the European Communities, Session 1983–4 *European Monetary System* 26 July 1983 HL 39. HMSO

Padoa-Schioppa T 1984 *Money, Economic Policy and Europe*. Commission of the European Communities.

van Ypersele J 1985 *The European Monetary System*. Commission of the European Communities

Chapter six

Commission of the EC *Annual Reports of the European Development Fund*. Office for Official Publications, Luxembourg

Keating M and Jones B 1985 *Regions of the European Community*. Clarendon Press

House of Lords 1982 12th Report – Select Committee on the European Communities, Session 1981–82 *Revision of the ERDF Regulations*. HMSO

House of Lords 1984 23rd Report – Select Committee on the European Communities. *ERDF*. HMSO

Pinder D 1983 *Regional Economic Development and Policy*. Allen and Unwin

Chapter seven

Cosgrove-Twitchett C 1981 *Harmonisation in the EEC*. Macmillan

Hall G (ed.) 1986 *European Industrial Policy*. Croom Helm

Pearce J and Sutton J 1986 (with R. Batchelor) *Protection and Industrial Policy in Europe*. Routledge and Kegan Paul

Sharp M (ed.) 1983 *Europe and the New Technologies*. Francis Pinter

Swann D 1983 *Competition and Industrial Policy in the European Community*. Methuen

Chapter eight

Anderson K & Tyers R 1984 EC grain and meat policies: effects on international prices trade and welfare *European Review of Agricultural Economics*, Vol 19

Commission of the European Communities 1987 *The Agricultural Situation in the Community 1986*. Office for Official Publications, Luxembourg

Commission of the European Communities 1987 *The Common Agricultural Policy and its Reform* (4th edn) European Documentation 1/1987. Office for Official Publications, Luxembourg

Fennell R 1985 A reconsideration of the objectives of the Common Agricultural Policy *Journal of Common Market Studies* XXIII (3)

Hill B E 1984 *The Common Agricultural Policy, Past Present and Future*. Methuen

Hill B E and Ingersent K A 1982 *An Economic Analysis of Agriculture*. Heinemann

House of Lords 1985 17th Report – Select Committee on the European Communities *The Reform of the Common Agricultural Policy* 30 July 1985 HL 237. HMSO

Chapter nine

Commission of the European Communities 1985 *The European Community Fisheries Policy*. Office for Official Publication, Luxembourg

Farnell J and Ellis J 1984 *In Search of a Common Fisheries Policy*. Gower

House of Lords 1984 1st Report – Select Committee on the European Communities *The Common Fisheries Policy* 11 Dec. 1984 HL 39. HMSO

Leigh M 1984 *European Integration and the Common Fisheries Policy*. Croom Helm

Shackleton M 1986 *The Politics of Fishing in Britain and France*. Gower

Wise M 1984 *The Common Fisheries Policy of the European Community*. Methuen

Chapter ten

Seers D and Vaitos C (eds) 1982 *The Second Enlargement of the EEC: The Integration of Unequal Partners*. Macmillan

Tsoukalis L (ed) 1981 *The European Community and its Mediterranean Enlargement*. Allen and Unwin

Yannopoulos G (ed.) 1986 *Greece and the EEC*. Macmillan

Williams A (ed.) 1984 *Southern Europe Transformed*. Harper and Row

Index

Key issues in Economics and Business
Series editors: Alan Griffiths, Keith Pye and Stuart Wall

Further books in this series include:

Government and the economy
K Bain and P G A Howells

The relationship between the public and private sectors is an area
of crucial importance in economics. The book deals clearly and
systematically with this key issue. Both macro- and micro-economic
aspects of this issue are examined, contrasting the views of economists throughout the first part of the book. In the second half,
outline answers to examination questions are given along with a
guide to further reading. The overall result is a valuable introduction to higher level studies in public sector economics and macro-
economics.

1987
0 582 29670 6

The problems of unemployment and inflation
P Hardwick

Unemployment and inflation are the two most significant problems
that have faced Britain and other western industrialised countries
in recent years. Among the issues which Philip Hardwick examines
are the social and economic effects of unemployment and inflation
and the recent policies implemented to deal with the problems.
Relevant examples from official statistics are provided throughout
the book.

1987
0 582 29661 7

Polish up your maths
G Bancroft and M Fletcher

This book aims to help all students who have begun a business
studies, economics, social science course or indeed any course with

a maths or statistics component in higher education. Concentrating on numeracy, graphical and simple algebraic skills, it can be used by students as a self-study guide. Exercises with solutions are provided along with a variety of illustrative examples.

1987
0 582 29721 4

International economics
G Donnelly

International economics examines the opportunities, problems and issues resulting from economic transactions between countries. The topics covered include, the principles and practice of international trade, the balance of payments, international liquidity and the multinationals. So that the student can take their studies further, the author gives along with his bibliography a guide to sources for obtaining data and information.

1987
0 582 29685 4